Chinese and Japanese in America

Also from Westphalia Press
westphaliapress.org

The Idea of the Digital University

Masonic Tombstones and Masonic Secrets

Eight Decades in Syria

Avant-Garde Politician

L'Enfant and the Freemasons

Baronial Bedrooms

Conflicts in Health Policy

Material History and Ritual Objects

Paddle Your Own Canoe

Opportunity and Horatio Alger

Careers in the Face of Challenge

Bookplates of the Kings

Collecting American Presidential Autographs

Misunderstood Children

Original Cables from the Pearl Harbor Attack

Social Satire and the Modern Novel

The Amenities of Book Collecting

The Genius of Freemasonry

A Definitive Commentary on Bookplates

James Martineau and Rebuilding Theology

No Bird Lacks Feathers

The Young Vigilantes

The Man Who Killed President Garfield

Anti-Masonry and the Murder of Morgan

Understanding Art

Homeopathy

Ancient Masonic Mysteries

Collecting Old Books

The Boy Chums Cruising in Florida Waters

The Thomas Starr King Dispute

Ivanhoe Masonic Quartettes

Lariats and Lassos

Mr. Garfield of Ohio

The Wisdom of Thomas Starr King

The French Foreign Legion

War in Syria

Naturism Comes to the United States

New Sources on Women and Freemasonry

Designing, Adapting, Strategizing in Online Education

Gunboat and Gun-runner

Meeting Minutes of Naval Lodge No. 4 F.A.A.M

Chinese and Japanese in America

The Immigration Controversies

Edited by Emory R. Johnson
& Chester Lloyd Jones

WESTPHALIA PRESS
An imprint of Policy Studies Organization

Westphalia Press
An imprint of Policy Studies Organization
1527 New Hampshire Ave., NW
Washington, D.C. 20036
info@ipsonet.org

ISBN-13: 978-1-63391-228-1
ISBN-10: 1633912280

Cover design by Jeffrey Barnes:
jbarnesdesign.com

Daniel Gutierrez-Sandoval, Executive Director
PSO and Westphalia Press

Updated material and comments on this edition
can be found at the Westphalia Press website:
www.westphaliapress.org

CHINESE AND JAPANESE IN AMERICA

THE ANNALS

OF THE

AMERICAN ACADEMY

OF

POLITICAL AND SOCIAL SCIENCE

ISSUED BI-MONTHLY

VOL. XXXIV, No. 2   SEPTEMBER, 1909

EDITOR: EMORY R. JOHNSON
ASSISTANT EDITOR: CHESTER LLOYD JONES
ASSOCIATE EDITORS: G. G. HUEBNER, CARL KELSEY, L. S. ROWE,
WALTER S. TOWER, FRANK D. WATSON, JAMES T. YOUNG

PHILADELPHIA
AMERICAN ACADEMY OF POLITICAL AND SOCIAL SCIENCE
36th and Woodland Avenue
1909

CONTENTS

PART I

THE ARGUMENT IN FAVOR OF ORIENTAL EXCLUSION

PAGE

CHINESE AND JAPANESE IMMIGRANTS—A COMPARISON..... 3
Chester H. Rowell, Editor "Fresno Republican," Fresno, Cal.

THE SUPPORT OF THE ANTI-ORIENTAL MOVEMENT......... 11
John P. Young, Editor San Francisco "Chronicle"

OPPOSITION TO ORIENTAL IMMIGRATION.................... 19
Walter Macarthur, Editor "Coast Seamen's Journal," San Francisco, Cal.

ORIENTAL VS. AMERICAN LABOR............................ 27
A. E. Yoell, Secretary Asiatic Exclusion League of North America, San Francisco, Cal.

MISUNDERSTANDING OF EASTERN AND WESTERN STATES REGARDING ORIENTAL IMMIGRATION.................... 37
Hon. Albert G. Burnett, Associate Justice, District Court of Appeals, Third Appellate District, Sacramento, Cal.

THE JAPANESE PROBLEM IN CALIFORNIA................... 42
Sidney G. P. Coryn, Of "The Argonaut," San Francisco, Cal.

A WESTERN VIEW OF THE RACE QUESTION................. 49
Hon. Francis G. Newlands, United States Senator from Nevada.

PART II

THE ARGUMENT AGAINST ORIENTAL EXCLUSION

UN-AMERICAN CHARACTER OF RACE LEGISLATION......... 55
Max J. Kohler, A.M., LL.B., Formerly Assistant United States District Attorney, New York.

REASONS FOR ENCOURAGING JAPANESE IMMIGRATION...... 74
John P. Irish, Naval Officer of Customs for the Port of San Francisco, Cal.

PAGE

MORAL AND SOCIAL INTERESTS INVOLVED IN RESTRICTING
ORIENTAL IMMIGRATION.................................. 80
Rev. Thomas L. Eliot, S.T.D., President, Board of Trustees of
Reed Institute, Portland Ore.

WHY OREGON HAS NOT HAD AN ORIENTAL PROBLEM........ 86
F. G. Young, Professor of Economics and Sociology, University
of Oregon, Eugene, Ore.

PART III

NATIONAL AND INTERNATIONAL ASPECTS OF THE EXCLUSION MOVEMENT

THE TREATY POWER: PROTECTION OF TREATY RIGHTS BY
FEDERAL GOVERNMENT 93
William Draper Lewis, Ph.D., Dean of the Law School, Univer-
sity of Pennsylvania, Philadelphia.

THE PROBLEM OF ORIENTAL IMMIGRATION IN THE STATE
OF WASHINGTON 109
Herbert H. Gowen, F.R.G.S., Lecturer on Oriental Literature,
University of Washington, Seattle, Wash.

THE EFFECT OF AMERICAN RESIDENCE ON JAPANESE..... 118
Baron Kentaro Kaneko, Tokio, Japan.

CHINESE LABOR COMPETITION ON THE PACIFIC COAST..... 120
Mary Roberts Coolidge, Formerly Associate Professor of
Sociology, Stanford University, Cal.; Author of "Chinese
Immigration" (in press).

THE LEGISLATIVE HISTORY OF EXCLUSION LEGISLATION... 131
Chester Lloyd Jones, Ph.D., Instructor in Political Science,
University of Pennsylvania, Philadelphia.

HOW CAN WE ENFORCE OUR EXCLUSION LAWS?............. 140
Marcus Braun, Immigrant Inspector, Department of Commerce
and Labor, Washington, D. C.

ENFORCEMENT OF THE CHINESE EXCLUSION LAW.......... 143
James Bronson Reynolds, New York.

Contents   v

PART IV

THE PROBLEM OF ORIENTAL IMMIGRATION
OUTSIDE OF AMERICA

PAGE

SOURCES AND CAUSES OF JAPANESE EMIGRATION.......... 157
    Yosaburo Yoshida, University of Wisconsin, Madison, Wis.

ORIENTAL IMMIGRATION INTO THE PHILIPPINES........... 168
    Russell McCulloch Story, A.M., Harvard University, Cam-
    bridge, Mass.

ORIENTAL LABOR IN SOUTH AFRICA....,..................... 175
    L. E. Neame, Johannesburg, South Africa; Author of "The
    Asiatic Danger in the Colonies."

JAPANESE IMMIGRATION INTO KOREA 183
    Thomas F. Millard, New York City; Author of "The New Far
    East" and "America and the Far Eastern Question."

THE EXCLUSION OF ASIATIC IMMIGRANTS IN AUSTRALIA.... 190
    Philip S. Eldershaw, B.A., and P. P. Olden, University Law
    School, Sydney, New South Wales.

PART ONE

The Argument in Favor of Oriental Exclusion

CHINESE AND JAPANESE IMMIGRANTS—A COMPARISON
BY CHESTER H. ROWELL,
EDITOR, "FRESNO REPUBLICAN," FRESNO, CAL.

THE SUPPORT OF THE ANTI-ORIENTAL MOVEMENT
BY JOHN P. YOUNG,
EDITOR, SAN FRANCISCO "CHRONICLE"

OPPOSITION TO ORIENTAL IMMIGRATION
BY WALTER MACARTHUR,
EDITOR, "COAST SEAMEN'S JOURNAL," SAN FRANCISCO, CAL.

ORIENTAL VERSUS AMERICAN LABOR
BY A. E. YOELL,
SECRETARY, ASIATIC·EXCLUSION LEAGUE OF NORTH AMERICA, SAN FRANCISCO, CAL.

MISUNDERSTANDING OF EASTERN AND WESTERN STATES REGARDING ORIENTAL IMMIGRATION
BY HON. ALBERT G. BURNETT,
ASSOCIATE JUSTICE, DISTRICT COURT OF APPEALS OF CALIFORNIA, THIRD APPELLATE DISTRICT, SACRAMENTO, CAL.

THE JAPANESE PROBLEM IN CALIFORNIA
BY SIDNEY G. P. CORYN,
OF "THE ARGONAUT," SAN FRANCISCO, CAL.

A WESTERN VIEW OF THE RACE QUESTION
BY HON. FRANCIS G. NEWLANDS,
UNITED STATES SENATOR FROM NEVADA

CHINESE AND JAPANESE IMMIGRANTS—
A COMPARISON

By CHESTER H. ROWELL,
Editor "Fresno Republican," Fresno, Cal.

If an off-hand comment on the more obvious facts of Chinese and Japanese immigration as they strike the average Californian is considered a sufficient response to the request of the editor of THE ANNALS for an article on this subject, it must be because precisely this off-hand view is one of the essential factors in any race problem.

It must always be remembered that the white American's standard of judging strange peoples is personal and unobjective. The average southern white man, for instance, is most favorably disposed toward a type of Negro objectively inferior,—the type, namely, which best fits the inferior status which the white man prefers the black man to occupy. In a part of California very familiar to the writer, there is a large Armenian and a large Russian immigration. The Armenian, who is generally a superior person, is unpopular because his success is for himself, in his own business. The Russian peasant, who is often an inferior person, is popular because his labor is useful to us, in our business. The same standard of judgment is applied to the Chinese and Japanese. Pinned down to an objective judgment of the races as such, the Californian would doubtless place the Japanese in the higher rank. He judges the Chinese by their coolie class, and regards them as an inferior race. But it is almost impossible to get the Californian to look at the question thus objectively. Ask the question, "Which race is superior?" and you get the subjective answer, "I find the Chinese more useful to me, in my business." Also, the American business man insists on judging men by business standards. The Chinese virtues are business virtues and the Japanese faults are business faults. Therefore, the Chinese are judged by their virtues and the Japanese by their faults.

Taking for the moment this biased viewpoint, we find the Chinese fitting much better than the Japanese into the status which the white American prefers them both to occupy—that of biped domestic animals in the white man's service. The Chinese coolie is the ideal industrial machine, the perfect human ox. He will transform less food into more work, with less administrative friction, than any other creature. Even now, when the scarcity of Chinese labor and the consequent rise in wages have eliminated the question of cheapness, the Chinese have still the advantage over all other servile labor in convenience and efficiency. They are patient, docile, industrious, and above all "honest" in the business sense that they keep their contracts. Also, they cost nothing but money. Any other sort of labor costs human effort and worry, in addition to the money. But Chinese labor can be bought like any other commodity, at so much a dozen or a hundred. The Chinese contractor delivers the agreed number of men, at the agreed time and place, for the agreed price, and if any one should drop out he finds another in his place. The men board and lodge themselves, and when the work is done they disappear from the employer's ken until again needed. The entire transaction consists in paying the Chinese contractor an agreed number of dollars for an agreed result. This elimination of the human element reduces the labor problem to something the employer can understand. The Chinese labor-machine, from his standpoint, is perfect.

But there are, of course, the additional standpoints of the merchant and the white laboring man. To the merchant the chief function of humanity is to "keep the money at home" and in circulation. The Chinaman spends his money with his own merchants, for Chinese goods, or sends it back to China directly. Therefore he is not a mercantile asset. In the old days, when the Chinese were sufficiently numerous and cheap to be real competitors, there was of course a violent labor-union opposition to them, most of which is now diverted to the Japanese, as the more immediate menace.

But all this is academic and historical. The Chinese are a disappearing problem. Most of those still remaining in America are old men. The few born in this country, and the more numerous ones smuggled in, are only a handful, and there are not now in California enough Chinese to do more than a small part of the servile labor which our transitional industrial condition could absorb. So long as California undertakes to do intensive farming on large estates, with a small population, so long will there be a demand for much more farm labor, at certain seasons, than the local industries can support or the local population absorb during the remainder of the year. Fortunately, there is a harvest of some sort going on in some part of California almost every month in the year, so that it is only necessary to organize the migration of this temporary labor to keep it continuously occupied. The problem of meeting this condition with organized white labor is difficult and has not yet been solved. Meantime, the Chinese have met ideally the requirements of the employing white farmer. But there are not enough of them left and in their search for a substitute the farmers have turned to the Japanese.

The Japanese are a very different people. As laborers they are less patient but quicker and brighter than the Chinese. In certain industries, particularly the thinning of sugar beets and the picking of raisin grapes, their short legs and ability to squat make them the most efficient workers in existence. A white man's efficiency is reduced very greatly when he has to squat. A Japanese can do as much work squatting as standing. Under the stimulus of "piece work," the Japanese work rapidly, but not carefully.

These differences, however, are minor. The one overshadowing contrast is this: The Chinese will keep a contract; the Japanese will not. Chinese business, like American business, is based on the assumption of the inviolability of contracts. Therefore the American and the Chinese can understand each other, on this point. But the Japanese seems to have no comprehension of the contract as a fundamental obligation, while the American cannot understand how a man can have any virtue who lacks this one. The Japanese contractor buys the fruit on the trees, as the Chinese used to do. The price goes down, and he refuses to understand how he could be bound by an agreement which has now ceased to be profitable. Japanese grape-pickers agree to pick a crop at a certain price. When the work is half done, there comes a chance to get a higher price elsewhere and they all decamp. There comes a sudden threat of rain in the drying season, and the trays must be "stacked" at once or the crop will be irreparably damaged. Instantly the cost of Japanese labor rises to blackmail prices, regardless of previous contracts. Of course there is such recourse as the law gives, but that is very little on a labor contract, and, generally, no legal obligation is worth much in business unless it is recognized also as a moral obligation. The Japanese does not recognize a contract as a moral obligation, and the American therefore assumes that he has no sense of any moral obligation. In an industrial system based on contract the Japanese must acquire a new sort of conscience, or he will remain an industrial misfit.

This of course is only the narrowly industrial view, chiefly that of the employing farmer. Socially, it is necessary to consider both the actual condition produced by the presence of Chinese and Japanese in moderate numbers, and the possible condition which would result if the bars were thrown down to the free immigration of either.

The Chinese live both by preference and by compulsion in "Chinatown," where they conduct their own affairs, independently of our laws and government, much as they do in China.

Adjoining Chinatown is usually the "tenderloin," and the whole district is the plague-spot of a California city. There is no law in Chinatown. The slave traffic is open and notorious, and slave pens, with bought slave girls peering through the barred windows, are a familiar sight. The most respected occupations of the leading Chinese citizens are gambling and lottery. As the laboring Chinese have become fewer, older and poorer, the games have turned to white men and Japanese for their victims. The Japanese rarely run gambling houses, but they are the chief frequenters of them, and lose much money. Chinese lotteries hold drawings twice a day, and tickets can be bought as cheaply as ten cents. Sometimes one small city will support a dozen lotteries. The tickets are peddled secretly, by the Chinese and by white cigar dealers and others, to American men and boys. In Chinatown the opium den or "hop joint" flourishes, and the opium-smoking white men who infest Chinatown are the dregs of creation. The governing bodies of Chinatown are the rival companies or "tongs," which enforce their decrees and settle their feuds by murder. There is a caste of professional hired murderers, or "highbinders," who are the executive arm of this peculiar government. The writer has seen the bodies of dead highbinders, after a tong war, stripped of actual chain armor, knife-proof and hatchet-proof. Chinese are sometimes convicted of murder, but there is never any telling whether you have convicted the right man. The Chinese whose word in a business obligation would be as good as a government bond, will perjure himself unblushingly on the witness stand. The jury-box estimate of Chinese testimony is that no Chinaman can be believed under oath. Chinese gambling joints are actual fortresses, with steel doors, sentries, and a labyrinth of secret exits. They are an open, fortified defiance of law, and are a source of almost universal police graft. An honest "Chinatown squad" is an iridescent dream. Sanitary conditions are unspeakable and sanitary regulations are unenforceable. Religion is represented by joss houses, where the coolie worshipper seeks which god will most cheaply grant his prayer for a winning lottery ticket.

There are decent men in Chinatown, but no moral leaders, and no civic sentiment, to enforce any moral obligations but business ones. These are absolute, and every Chinese pays all his debts by the time of the annual New Year festivities. Superstition is universal and gross, and the numerous devils are the only power feared, except the tongs. Dead men are greatly honored, but a dying man is thrust into the dead-house to starve, supplied with opium, but with nothing else. Chinese clothing, food, customs and standards are universal, and a Californian Chinatown is simply a miniature section of Canton, transported bodily. The Chinese are not part of American life, and conform to American standards only in the single respect of recognizing the obligation of a business contract.

The Japanese in the beginning congregate on the borders of Chinatown, but they build better and cleaner houses and admit some air to them. They adopt American clothing at once, and American customs very rapidly. As they grow in numbers and prosperity, they provide themselves with recreation—good and bad. They go to the Chinese gambling houses and to the Buddhist temples and Christian missions. Pool and billiard rooms, with their good and bad points, are liberally patronized. The general aspect of life is cheerful and attractive, and the Japanese themselves, from the highest to the lowest, are a delightfully polite and genial people. Even the "cockyness" that has followed the Russian war has not obliterated their personal likableness. In every relation but a business one they are charming. They develop a civic sense, public spirit, and moral leadership. When the Chinese gambling joints debauch the Japanese young men, the Buddhist priest, the Christian missionary and the president of the Japanese Reform Association call on the mayor to protest. But when asked whether the Japanese houses of prostitution should not be suppressed also, they shake their heads. Prostitution is a most characteristic Japanese industry, and there appears to be no moral sentiment against it. The women themselves are under less social ostracism than the women of corresponding class of other races, and they appear also to be less personally degraded. You seen no obscene pictures and no flaunting of vulgarity in a Japanese house of prostitution. In some places, these facts are giving the Japanese an approximate monopoly of this evil.

But the Japanese do not confine themselves to "Japtown," nor permit the white man to determine the limits of their residence. They buy up town and country property, and wherever they settle the white man moves out. In Sacramento they have completely occupied what was formerly one of the best business districts. The process is simple. A Japanese buys a fine corner location, paying for it whatever price he must. Then he gets all the rest of the block very cheaply, for the white owners and tenants will not stay. In the country, wherever the Japanese rent or buy land in any quantities, white men evacuate. The Vaca Valley, one of the richest and most beautiful spots in California, is the most notable example. Similiar beginnings have been made elsewhere. In business they do not confine themselves to their own people. In Fowler, California, for instance, one of the leading department stores, doing a general business with Americans, is owned by Sumida Bros. In San Francisco there is a Japanese daily newspaper, with a modern plant and a large circulation and business. It was the first newspaper in San Francisco to resume publication with its own building and plant after the fire.

The Japanese are energetic, versatile and adaptable. Many of them attend the high schools and universities, to secure a first-class American education. These students frequently work, after hours, as house servants in American families, partly to support themselves and partly to supplement their American academic education with an American domestic education. As servants they are intelligent, accommodating, competent and unstable. As in everything else, their one weakness is their failure to recognize the obligation of a contract. They will leave, without notice or consideration, on the slightest provocation. Chinese servants, such of them as there are left, are more generally professional servants, who make the work a permanent business, and expect high wages.

Magnify these conditions indefinitely, and it is not hard to foresee the result of any general admission of immigrants of either

race. Chinese will not assimilate with American life, and Americans
refuse to assimilate with Japanese. The great danger of the "yellow
peril" is its enormous size. With less than two million white men in
California, and more than four hundred million Chinese in China,
just across the way, the very smallest overflow from that limitless
reservoir would swamp our Pacific Coast. If it is impossible for
two million white men, in an American state, to enforce American
laws on a dwindling few thousand Chinese, American institutions
would be simply obliterated by any considerable influx of Chinese.
A very few years of unrestricted Chinese immigration would leave
California, American only in the sense in which Hongkong is English. Fortunately, on this question, American policy is fixed, and is
for the present in our hands. China is powerless to protest, whether
we deal justly or unjustly, and the dwindling remnant of Chinese
present few occasions for personal or diplomatic friction. The Chinese
problem is easy, so long as our present policy continues. Under any
other policy, it would straightway overwhelm us. No possible
immediate industrial demand could justify letting down the bars
to Chinese immigration in even the slightest degree. Those industries
which cannot be developed and those resources which cannot be
exploited without Chinese labor must simply be left undeveloped and
unexploited—unless we are willing to sacrifice American civilization permanently to industrial exploitation temporarily, on the whole
Pacific Coast.

The Chinese problem is approaching its end, unless we reopen
it. The Japanese problem is only beginning, and the end is not
wholly within our control. For the present, there are no more
Japanese in the country than we can safely utilize, and the number,
under the restrictive policy of Japan, appears to be decreasing.
This is excellent, so long as it lasts. But it can last, in peace and
amity, only so long as Japan wills, and Japanese sensitiveness constantly tends to magnify the smallest provocations into international issues. Industrially, we can utilize some Japanese, but internationally we cannot guarantee even one Japanese against the
possible chances of American hoodlumism. With the issue, not
probably of peace (for war is the remotest of contingencies), but
of amity in the hands of any rowdy boy who chooses to smash a
Japanese window, the present Japanese exclusion arrangement is in
the unstablest equilibrium. A momentary wave of demagogy, in

Japanese politics, a chance street fight in the San Francisco slums, and the whole agreement might be jeopardized. Then we should be forced to the alternative of Japanese exclusion by our own initiative, with all its difficulties and possibilities of complication.

But let no American who realizes what it would mean to the South to turn back the wheels of history and decree that there should never have been a race problem there, consider for a moment the possibility of importing another and harder one on our Pacific Coast. There is no right way to solve a race problem except to stop it before it begins. Every possible solution of the Negro problem is a wrong one, but we can at least let each generation determine which wrong it will commit, and take the consequences, with respect to that permanently impossible problem. No such possibility opens with respect to a race problem where the other race would determine its own view of its own rights, and be backed by a powerful and jealous nation in maintaining them. The Pacific Coast is the frontier of the white man's world, the culmination of the westward migration which is the white man's whole history. It will remain the frontier so long as we guard it as such; no longer. Unless it is maintained there, there is no other line at which it can be maintained without more effort than American government and American civilization are able to sustain. The multitudes of Asia are already awake, after their long sleep, as the multitudes of Europe were when our present flood of continental immigration began. We know what could happen, on the Asiatic side, by what did happen and is happening on the European side. On that side we have survived, and such of the immigration as we have not assimilated for the present we know is assimilable in the future. But against Asiatic immigration we could not survive. The numbers who would come would be greater than we could encyst, and the races who would come are those which we could never absorb. The permanence not merely of American civilization, but of the white race on this continent, depends on our not doing, on the Pacific side, what we have done on the Atlantic Coast. For the present, the situation as to both Chinese and Japanese immigration is satisfactory. But to relax the present policy, even for a brief interval, would be to load ourselves with a burden which all eternity could not again throw off and all our vitality could not withstand. There is no other possible national menace at all to be compared with this.

THE SUPPORT OF THE ANTI-ORIENTAL MOVEMENT

By John P. Young,
Editor San Francisco "Chronicle."

It is occasionally necessary to remind the people of the American Union who live on the eastern side of the Rocky Mountains that they have the bad habit of forming hasty judgments concerning matters with which they are not particularly familiar. They have done so repeatedly in cases in which they might have fairly deferred to the experience of the Far West. A notable instance was the attitude of the East on the subject of Chinese immigration. At first the sentiment of the older section of the Union was averse to any restriction being placed on the importation or immigration of Chinese laborers; but in the end, after extended investigations, Congress decided that expediency and justice demanded that the unassimilable Oriental be excluded.

A brief reference to the agitation which finally resulted in the passage of what is known as the Chinese exclusion act will help the reader to divest himself of the opinion prevalent in the Eastern States that the objection to Oriental immigration is due to the machinations of the labor unions on the Pacific Coast and does not represent the sentiment or wishes of the people at large. This assertion was freely made during the period when exclusion was being discussed by Congress. It was based on assertions made by a small number of interested persons, who believed that the interests of California would be best subserved by maintaining intact the large individual holdings of land which could only be profitably worked by cheap and docile laborers, such as experience had taught them the Chinese would be if they could be brought into the country in sufficiently large numbers, or by the small contingent which thought that a servile class was needed to make life endurable.

So confused was the evidence regarding the desirability of excluding the Chinese that as early as July 27, 1868, Congress passed a joint resolution directing a thorough investigation of the subject. A Congressional committee visited the Pacific Coast and made exhaustive inquiries and subsequently made a report which while in the main favoring the contention of those urging exclusion did not produce any affirmative legislation until 1879, when Congress passed an act excluding Chinese laborers, which was vetoed by President Hayes.

How largely he was influenced to take this adverse course by the mistaken belief of Eastern people that the opposition to Chinese immigration came wholly from the followers of Dennis Kearney it would be difficult to say, but it is a fact that the opinion was generally entertained at the East that the demand was the result of the Sand Lot agitation, and that there was no unanimity of sentiment in favor of putting up the bars. This belief was fostered by the publication of articles in the Eastern press asserting that the development of California was absolutely dependent upon Chinese labor, and that without an abundant supply of it there would be an end to the progress of the state.

To put an end to this false impression the Legislature of California directed that a test vote should be taken at a general election. In conformity with this resolution, at an election held on September 3, 1879, the voters of California cast their ballots "For" and "Against Chinese Immigration." The result was that in a poll of a little over 162,000 votes, 161,405 were "against" and only 638 "for" Chinese immigration. As the ballot was absolutely secret this overwhelming vote "Against Chinese Immigration" showed that the people of California were practically a unit in favor of exclusion. The evidence was so conclusive that further resistance on the part of the East ceased and in 1882 an act was passed suspending Chinese immigration for ten years. This was subsequently amended, making the exclusion of the Chinese laboring class perpetual.

The recital of these facts ought to warn the Eastern critics of the anti-Japanese immigration movement on this coast that they may be in error in assuming that the attitude of the Pacific Coast on the subject has been inspired by labor agitators, and that the demand for exclusion does not represent the sentiment of all classes in California and of the other states on the Pacific Coast. As a matter of fact, such an assumption is wholly erroneous. The movement did not have its origin in labor circles. As will be shown, the labor leaders had to be taught that they were confronted with a graver menace than that which the Chinese exclusion law averted. They did not take up the matter actively until the legislature had unanimously adopted a resolution memorializing Congress on the subject and asking that body to adopt laws to stem the threatened flood of Japanese coolies.

The first warning note came from the San Francisco "Chronicle." On February 23, 1905, that journal began the publication of a series of articles the scope of which was stated in the introduction to the opening paper of the series which was prepared by a writer after an extended inquiry which covered the ground fully, embracing every phase of the question subsequently discussed. These were the words used:

> In the accompanying article the "Chronicle" begins a careful and conservative exposition of the problem which is no longer to be ignored—the Japanese question. It has been but slightly touched upon heretofore; now it is pressing upon California and upon the entire United States as heavily and contains as much of a menace as the matter of Chinese immigration ever did, if, indeed, it is not more serious, socially, industrially and from an international standpoint. It demands consideration. This article shows that since 1880, when the census noted a Japanese population in California of only eighty-six, not less than 35,000 of the little brown men have come to the state and remained here. At the present day the number of Japanese in the United States is very conservatively estimated at 100,000. Immigration is increasing steadily, and, as in the case of the Chinese, it is the worst she has that Japan sends to us. The Japanese is no more assimilable than the Chinese and he is not less adaptable in learning quickly how to do the white man's work, and how to get the job for himself by offering his labor for less than a white man can live on.

In entering upon this crusade the "Chronicle" did not do so without deliberation. Nine years earlier the writer of this article had prepared for the "Chronicle" a monograph on the subject of Japanese competition, in gathering data for which he had become deeply impressed with the capabilities of the people of the island empire and took the liberty of presenting their claims to be considered seriously. At that time the people of the East had not overcome the habit of regarding the Japanese in the light in which they were presented in Gilbert and Sullivan's opera of "The Mikado," but to the author the facts presented themselves differently and he remarked.

> It would be a gross blunder to class a people as barbarous who had reached such an artistic and industrial development as that attained by the Japanese. It is unwise to underrate the qualities of a competitor . . . The

Western invader did not find a semi-civilized people in Japan; he merely found a civilization differing from his own, and with the customary contemptuousness of a conquerer he underrated it.

The monograph sketched the progress made in the various industrial arts and the writer unhesitatingly predicted that Japan would become a formidable rival of Western manufacturing nations. It attracted the attention of a United States Senator, who found something in its argument to support a contention he was making at the time and he caused it to be printed as a Senate document. Curiously enough, the chief facts and the predictions concerning the development of the Japanese manufacturing industry were ignored, while a mere side issue, that relating to the advantages possessed by Japan while on a silver basis, was animadverted upon and disputed. At the time Britons and Americans were so engrossed with the idea that the Orient was especially created for them to exploit that they were inclined to treat such predictions as vain imaginings. Since then they have had abundant evidence that the predictions were not unwarranted, for Japan has become a formidable competitor in many fields which Westerners until recently never dreamed would be invaded by the race they assumed to be inferior.

The "Chronicle" never had any illusions on this score. The position of San Francisco in relation to the Orient made its editors observant of the transpacific peoples and qualified them to form a more accurate judgment than that inspired by a desire to exploit, and the arrogant feeling of superiority which make publications like the New York "Independent" reproach Californians with being cowardly because they shrink from the possibilities of a competition with a race fully as capable as our own and having the added advantage of being inured by centuries of self-denial to a mode of life to which we do not wish to conform, even if we had the ability to do so.

When the "Chronicle" on February 23, 1905, sounded its warning, it did so because it believed that an inundation of Japanese would result in a competition as effective domestically as the output of its manufacturing industries is becoming internationally. It did not assume that the laborer was the only person affected. It recognized that the introduction of large numbers of the working classes would result in edging out the white worker, but it perceived that the victory over the latter would pave the way to a complete orientaliza-

tion of the Pacific Coast states and territories. The recognition may
be regarded as an admission of inferiority; it has been sneeringly
alluded to as a confession of that kind. But sneers do not change
facts, and if it is true—and experience teaches us that it is—that the
Japanese, by superior virtues or the practice of economies to which
we cannot or will not accustom ourselves, can drive us out of business, we would be fools to refuse to take precautions against such a
result.

It is necessary to dwell on this phase to show that Pacific Coast
antipathy to Japanese immigration is not the result of the fear of
workingmen, and that the agitation was not the inspiration of labor
unions. It was sound arguments and columns of facts that aroused
the people to action. The first publication on the subject, as already
stated, appeared on February 23, 1905. On the ensuing 1st of
March, the Senate of California, by a unanimous vote, passed the
following concurrent resolution:

> *Resolved, by the Senate, the Assembly concurring,* That in view of the
> facts and the reasons aforesaid (recited in the preamble), and of many others
> that might be stated, we, as representatives of the people of the State of
> California, do earnestly and strenuously ask and request, and in so far as
> it may be proper, demand, for the protection of the people of this state
> and for the proper safeguarding of their interests, that action be taken
> without delay, by treaty or otherwise, as may be most expeditious and advan-
> tageous, tending to limit within reasonable bounds and diminish to a marked
> degree the further immigration of Japanese laborers into the United States.
> That they, our Senators and Representatives in Congress, be and are hereby
> requested and directed to bring the matters aforesaid to the attention of the
> President and Department of State.

On the 4th of March the assembly, without a dissenting voice,
concurred, and the resolution, as adopted, was sent to Washington.
The representatives of California in Congress complied promptly
with the demand of the legislature. Up to the date of the adoption
of the concurrent resolution by the Senate no labor organization in
San Francisco or on the Pacific Coast had expressed itself on the
subject. The first intimation that the public had that labor was
interested was the passage of the following resolution by the San
Francisco Labor Council on the night of March 2d:

> *Resolved,* That we earnestly request the Labor Council to take such
> steps as it may deem necessary to promote agitation of this question among

the unions of the city and state by resolutions and mass meetings if necessary, for the purpose of strengthening the hands of our representatives in Congress and impressing upon them and all other representatives the necessity of passing adequate laws, and that the agitation be kept up until the object is attained.

There was nothing incendiary in this resolution; it was a matter-of-fact pronouncement made by men who understood the subject, and who acted promptly when their attention was called to the menace. At the time it was made there was no excitement, nor were there any exhibitions of race prejudice. The first mention of a possible objection to the presence of Japanese in the public schools was made in an article published in the "Chronicle" on March 5, 1905, which contained these words: "Precise statistics do not seem to be available, but a careful estimate made some six months ago showed the presence of over 1,000 Japanese pupils in the schools of San Francisco alone." In the same connection attention was called to Article X, Section 1662, of school law of California, which provided for the establishment of an Oriental public school for Japanese, Chinese or Corean children.

On the 5th of May, 1905, two months after the adoption of the concurrent resolution by the legislature, the Board of Education of San Francisco made the following declaration:

Resolved, That the Board of Education is determined in its efforts to effect the establishment of separate schools for Chinese and Japanese pupils, not only for the purpose of relieving the congestion at present prevailing in our schools, but also for the higher end that our children should not be placed in any position where their youthful impressions may be affected by association with pupils of the Mongolian race.

This declaration attracted very little attention at the time. If the Japanese protested against it, the fact was not made public. It is probable that they recognized the justice of some of the arguments urged in favor of segregation, and if they had not been inspired to act otherwise it is reasonably certain nothing would have been heard from them on the subject. At any rate, nothing came of the declaratory resolution, and it might have been completely ignored by the board making it had not the conflagration of 1906 destroyed many of the schools in the city and made it a difficult problem to take care of the white children of San Francisco. It was not until October 11, 1906, that active steps were taken to carry out the provision of the state law. On that date the Board of Education of San Francisco adopted the following:

Resolved, That in accordance with Article X, Section 1662, of the School Law of California, principals are hereby directed to send all Chinese, Japanese or Corean children to the Oriental Public School, situated on the south side of Clay street, between Powell and Mason streets, on and after Monday, October 15, 1906.

It is doubtful whether this declaration would have incited the Japanese to protest had not the authorities at Washington objected. Immediately after its publication Victor H. Metcalf, then Secretary of the Navy, was sent to the coast to make an investigation, and he made a report to the President, the effect of which was to create the impression at the East that the Japanese on the coast were the objects of continuous persecution. Trifling affairs, which scarcely merited the attention of a police court, were magnified into matters of international importance. The "Chronicle" at the time took occasion to comment on the unfairness of his presentation, and it has since been explained that he was only expected to see one side of the case. In short, ex-President Roosevelt appeared to be seeking for matter upon which to base the most extraordinary attack ever made upon a section of the American Union. In his message to Congress, delivered in December, 1906, he threatened California with an armed invasion if it did not abandon its recalcitrant attitude, and he pictured a condition of affairs as existing here which, had it really existed, would have been shameful; but as it did not, he merely convicted himself of adding another to the long list of his hasty judgments.

It is not the purpose of this article to disprove the assertion that the Japanese in California are the victims of race hatred, or that they are oppressed because they are Japanese. It would be a waste of space to dwell on the subject, for the evidence is overwhelming that in all their ordinary relations with the people they are as well treated as any other foreigners in our midst. Hoodlums make assaults upon other foreigners, but nothing is heard of them, but the Japanese insist upon converting every difficulty in which they become involved into an international affair. During the waiters' strike in this city, Frenchmen, Germans, Italians and other foreigners suffered, but they did not appeal to their governments for redress.

It is only the Japanese who do so, and they make their appeals becauses they considered themselves as subjects of the Mikado, whom they have been led to believe exercises as much influence on this side of the Pacific as he does in his own empire.

My object is merely to make clear that the anti-Japanese immigration movement in California did not originate in labor circles, although, as is quite natural, the workingmen are a unit in their opposition to the introduction of a non-assimilable race. Despite the impression to the contrary which has been produced by the ill-considered assertions of a few men, the opposition is very general, and there is not the slightest doubt that if a vote on exclusion were taken it would, after a brief campaign of education, be as nearly unanimous as that cast against Chinese immigration in 1879, when less than four-tenths of one per cent of the qualified electors of California voted in favor of continuing the admission of Chinese laborers. The motives that contributed to that result would again operate in the case of the Japanese and in a much more powerful manner, because the people are profoundly convinced that only by their exclusion can the white man's civilization be preserved on the Pacific coast.

But meanwhile we pay the Japanese the compliment of being reasonable beings and not desirous of becoming involved in a conflict with the United States. They have shown this disposition from the beginning, despite the attempts to exaggerate certain political movements into professions of hostility. The people of the Pacific coast understand the situation, and do not seriously regard the war talk so frequently indulged in by Washington correspondents. They believe that President Roosevelt used the alleged grievances of the Japanese as a bogy to secure consideration for his plans for a bigger navy, and while he from the wilds of Africa is sending out warnings and advice to get ready to repel an invasion of Japanese warships the people of San Francisco and of the Pacific coast generally, have been showering courtesies on visiting Japanese ships, fully convinced that pleasant international relations can be maintained with Japan even if we do insist that it is unwise to bring two unassimilable races in close and dangerous contact.

OPPOSITION TO ORIENTAL IMMIGRATION

By Walter Macarthur,

Editor "Coast Seamen's Journal," San Francisco, California.

The opposition to Oriental immigration is justified upon the single ground of race. Whether the incompatibility of the peoples of Asia and America can be attributed to race repulsion, race antipodalism, or race prejudice, one indisputable ground of race conflict remains, namely, that of race difference. The race difference between these peoples is radical and irreconcilable, because it reaches to the most fundamental characteristics of each. It is not a matter of tongue, of color, or of anatomy, although in each of these respects the difference is very clearly marked, but of morality and intellect.

Only upon the race ground can we comprehend the real nature and dimensions of the subject. Considered from this standpoint, exclusion follows as the inescapable law of our national safety and progress. Considered from any other standpoint—that is, with any other point as the basis of reasoning—the subject becomes involved in matters of detail, which, being in themselves matters of dispute, lead only to interminable discussion. Recognizing the race aspect of the subject as the main ground of exclusion, the minor grounds, such as those of an economic or political nature, serve to reinforce the argument as so many corollaries.

The instinct of race preservation is the strongest impulse of mankind in the aggregate. No incidents in history are more familiar than the successive Asiatic invasions of Europe. The influence of these invasions, persisting to the present day, is equally well known.

Nearly five hundred years before the birth of Christ the Asiatic invasion of Europe was successfully challenged by Miltiades on the field of Marathon. Ten years later Leonidas died at Thermopylae while defending the "ashes of his fathers and the temples of his gods." The success of the Persian king, Xerxes, on that occasion was but the forerunner of his defeat in the same year by Themistocles at Salamis,

"When on these seas the sons of Athens conquered
The various powers of Asia."

The two great battles between Alexander and Darius (334-331 B. C.), resulting in the destruction of the Persian monarchy, are so many incidents in the same great struggle. The conquest of a great part of southeastern Europe by the Huns in the fifth century, the defeat of Attila at Chalons, and the settlement of his followers in the country now known as Hungary, left the world the heritage of a mixed race that forms a constant menace to its peace. The invasion of Asia Minor and the Balkan States by the Ottoman Turks in the eleventh century laid the fairest region of Europe under tribute to Asia and demoralized the Caucasian race in that region, thus giving rise to that admixture of peoples, the type of which is commonly referred to as "unspeakable."

The best known and most far-reaching of these invasions is that which began under the leadership of Genghiz Khan, in the thirteenth century, followed by that of Timur, in the fourteenth century, and continuing at intervals until the sixteenth century. For 224 years, namely, from 1238 to 1462, the Mongols were supreme in Russia. The immediate result of the struggle to drive the Mongols back over the Urals was the establishment of an autocratic government, of which the present reigning house of Russia is the lineal descendant. A further result is seen in the Tartar strain that runs through the people of southern and eastern Russia, the utilization of which, as in the case of the Cossacks, is responsible for much of the cruelty perpetrated upon the people of "White Russia."

Of a kind with these historical race wars is the Arab invasion of Spain, in 711, and the subsequent incursions into France. Until 1492, a period of nearly eight hundred years, the Moors remained in control of almost the whole of Spain. The success of the Moorish invaders in France was short-lived. They were met and defeated by Charles Martel, at Tours in 732. In a few years they were driven to the southward of the Pyrenees, and thus a limit was set to the advance of Asia in Europe.

The persistence of these invasions, and the ferocity that marked their conduct, indicate quite clearly the irresponsible nature of the conflict between the races. The conflict is irrepressible because it arises from a difference in the nature of the races. To describe this difference in so many words is a task the success of which must, of course, be limited by the ability to define and express the respective race instincts. Certain characteristics of the Asiatic and Caucasian races are sufficiently manifest to permit of contrast in terms of general comprehension. Such a contrast was drawn by United States Senator Perkins, in a speech on the Exclusion Law, in 1902, in which he said:

> Personal freedom, the home, education, Christian ideals, respect for law and order are found on one side, and on the other the traffic in human flesh, domestic life which renders a home impossible, a desire for only that knowledge which may be at once coined into dollars, a contempt for our religion as new, novel and without substantial basis, and no idea of the meaning of law other than a regulation to be evaded by cunning or by bribery.

As exemplifying the attitude of the Chinese toward Christianity, the following, from a letter written four years ago by Ambassador Wu, is significant:

> There is no objection to Christianity as a theory, but as something practical it is entirely out of the question. We tried such a system in China five or six thousand years ago, but we had to get a philosophy that the people could live up to. No people ever obey the precepts of the Christian religion; the whole system is a failure. Theoretically it is all right, but practically it is a failure.

A distinguished Japanese recently described Christianity as "not a religion, but a commercial system." This attitude of mind may account for the fact that the number of Chinese converts to Christianity amounted to little more than 1,000 after sixteen years' labor of about a hundred missionaries at the five treaty ports.[1] The number of such converts is still hardly more than nominal. It is authoritatively stated that not more than one per cent of the Japanese have embraced Christianity.

> It is the superstitious that need religion, says the Japan "Mail." With no god to worship and no immortal soul to think about, educated people can pass their lives very pleasantly in the enjoyment that nature and art have bestowed upon them. Of what use to them is the religion that satisfies the uncultured mind?

[1]"Religious Condition of the Chinese," by Rev. Joseph Edkins, 1859.

United States Senator Money, in a recent speech on the Negro question, thus describes the race from which the American people have sprung:

The characteristics of these people were their personal love of liberty, their high spirit of adventure, their willingness to take all responsibility, their ability to rise to the demand of every occasion, and one of the grandest features of it all was their profound respect and love for women.

The well-known views of Herbert Spencer, concerning the effects of race admixture, are highly pertinent at this juncture. In his letter to Baron Kentaro Kaneko, Spencer said:

I have for the reasons indicated entirely approved of the regulations which have been established in America for restricting Chinese immigration, and had I the power I would restrict them to the smallest possible amount, my reasons for this decision being that one of two things must happen. (If the Chinese are allowed to settle extensively in America they must either, if they remain non-mixed, form a subjective race standing in the position, if not of slaves, yet of a class approaching slaves, or, if they mix, they must form a bad hybrid. In either case, supposing the immigration to be large, immense social mischief must arise and eventually social disorganization. *The same thing would happen if there should be any considerable mixture of European races with the Japanese.*

Lafcadio Hearn, in his "Life and Letters," casts a strong light upon the alleged assimilability of the Japanese, as follows:

Here is an astounding fact. The Japanese child is as close to you as the European child—perhaps closer, and sweeter, because infinitely more natural and naturally refined. Cultivate his mind, and the more it is cultivated the farther you push him from you. Why? Because here the race antipodalism shows itself. As the Oriental thinks naturally to the left where we think to the right, the more you cultivate him the more he will think in the opposite direction from you. . . . My conclusion is that the charm of Japanese life is largely the charm of childhood, and that the most beautiful of all race childhoods is passing into an adolescence which threatens to prove repulsive.

Speaking of the difference in the circumstances of race admixture in the United States and in other countries, and noting the advantage of the former in the fact that "a single language became dominant from the time of the earliest permanent settlement," Professor John R. Commons, of the University of Wisconsin, says:[3]

[3] "Races and Immigrants in America."

This is essential, for it is not physical amalgamation that unites man-kind; it is mental community. To be great a nation need not be of one blood, it must be of one mind. Racial inequality and inferiority are fundamental only to the extent that they prevent mental and moral assimilation. If we think together we can act together, and the organ of common thought and action is common language. Through the prism of this noble instrument of the human mind all other instruments focus their powers of assimilation upon the new generations as they come forth from the disunited immigrants.

It is precisely in "mental community" that the Asiatic is most lacking. It is said that the Japanese language contains no words synonymous with "sin" and "home," presumably because the Japanese have no conception of either. They do not think in terms of Caucasian or Christian morality.

The economic and political grounds of opposition to Asiatic immigration have their bases in the race question. The Asiatic is a cheap laborer because he lacks the racial impulse that makes for the maintenance of a high standard of living. He is a menace to free government because he lacks the inspiration of personal liberty.

Referring to the attitude of the American working class toward the labor of alien races, Professor Commons says:[a]

They were compelled to admit that though they themselves had been immigrants, or the children of immigrants, they were now denying to others what had been a blessing to them. Yet they were able to set forward one argument which our race problems are every day more and more showing to be sound. *The future of American democracy is the future of the American wage-earner. To have an enlightened and patriotic citizenship we must protect the wages and standard of living of those who constitute the bulk of the citizens.* . . . For it must be observed in general that race antagonism occurs on the same competitive level. What appear often to be religious, political, and social animosities are economic at bottom, and the substance of the economic struggle is the advantage which third parties get when competitors hold each other down. . . . It was the poor white who hated the negro and fled from his presence to the hills and the frontier, or sank below his level, despised by white and black. In times of freedom and reconstruction it is not the great landholder or employer that leads in the exhibition of race hostility, but the small farmer or wage-earner. The one derives a profit from the presence of the negro—the other loses his job or his farm.

While it is true that ordinarily "race antagonism occurs on

[a] "Races and Immigrants in America."

the same competitive level," thus lending color to the assumption that the race problem is "economic at bottom," too great emphasis is placed upon the economic phase. Of course, Oriental immigration is induced largely by economic conditions. But were Orientals attracted to this country by other reasons entirely, and were they to occupy a different place in the social and economic order, the race problem would still persist.

It is frequently contended that an illimitable supply of Asiatic labor would be a good thing for the American workman, by relieving him of those forms of labor which are in their nature disagreeable and poorly paid. This view is sometimes expressed in the form of an analogy between the cheap laborer and the labor-saving tool. This contention is a complete reversal of the tradition concerning the "dignity of labor." The American workman, skilled or unskilled, is not yet ready to accept the classification of labor of any kind as a "tool" in the hands of other men. The American people are not yet ready to assume that certain forms of labor are less honorable, or "dignified," than others, and therefore less entitled to share the responsibilities and enjoy the respect of common citizenship.[4]

The number of Japanese at present in the United States is estimated at 130,000, of whom 60,000 are located in California, a decrease of 5,000 in that state during the past year, due to eastward migration.[5] The number of Japanese in Hawaii is 72,000.[6] The number of Chinese in California is estimated at 35,000; in the United States, 300,000.[7] The Japanese own and control several of the most fertile parts of California and are rapidly making themselves felt in almost every branch of trade and commerce, not merely as cheap-labor "tools," but as active business competitors. The Asiatic population of Hawaii now exceeds that of the combined Caucasian and native elements.[8] The same condition exists among the children in the public schools,[9] and the increase of native-born

---

[4]Cheap labor may hinder industrial development. "Great estates ruined Italy." On the same principle it is said that "Spanish grants and coolie labor" have hindered the development of California.

[5]Statistics of Asiatic Exclusion League, San Francisco.

[6]Report of Governor Frear, 1909.

[7]United States Senate Report 776, February, 1902.

[8]Bulletin of the Bureau of Labor, No. 66, September, 1906.

[9]J. Kuhio Kalanianaole, Hawaiian Delegate to Congress.

Asiatics in that territory already threatens American supremacy in the political field.

With the progress of industrial development in Asia, involving a radical change in the national habit of life, from that of "sacrificing production to population," as under a hand-labor system of industry, to one of "sacrificing population to production," as under a machine system of industry, it is inevitable that the struggle for an outlet for the surplus population must constantly become more severe. Unless checked by exclusion laws, the forced migration of the disemployed of Asia will follow the line of least resistance, namely, toward the western shores of the United States.

The demand for Asiatic exclusion originated in the earliest period of American development on the Pacific Coast. In 1852, the California legislature imposed a tax upon Chinese miners. Subsequently other state measures were adopted as a means of protecting American labor from competition with Chinese. These measures were declared invalid, as being beyond the authority of the state. In 1877, the California legislature passed an act calling for a vote of the people on the question of Chinese immigration. The vote was taken on September 3, 1879, and resulted in 833 votes in favor and 154,638 against the admission of Chinese. The adoption of the Burlingame Treaty, in 1868, followed by various acts of Congress enacted in 1882, 1884, 1888, 1892 and 1902, marks the respective stages of the federal legislation culminating in the total exclusion of Chinese, other than "merchants, teachers, students and travelers for pleasure or curiosity."

In 1854, Victoria and New South Wales, Australia, enacted Asiatic restriction laws. At present Asiatics are practically excluded from Canada, Australia and New Zealand by a prohibitive head tax of $500. In the two last-named countries this tax is imposed upon all persons not of white color and blood, even though they be British subjects.

The principles of exclusion and the means of attaining that object are very well set forth by United States Senator Newlands, in the following terms:[10]

History teaches that it is impossible to make a homogeneous people by a juxtaposition of races differing in color upon the same soil. Race tolerance, under such conditions, means race amalgamation, and this is unde-

[10]Letter of Senator Newlands to the Legislature of Nevada, February 8, 1909.

sirable. Race intolerance means, ultimately, race war and mutual destruction, or the reduction of one of the races to servitude. The admission of a race of a different color, in a condition of industrial servitude, is foreign to our institutions, which demand equal rights to all within our jurisdiction. The competition of such a race would involve industrial disturbance and hostility, requiring the use of a large armed force to maintain peace and order, with the probability that the nation representing the race thus protected would never be satisfied that the means employed were adequate. The presence of the Chinese, who are patient and submissive, would not create as many complications as the presence of the Japanese, whose strong and virile qualities would constitute an additional factor of difficulty. *Our friendship, therefore, with Japan, for whose territorial and race integrity the American people have stood in active sympathy in all her 'truggles, demands that this friendship should not be put to the test by bringing two such powerful races of such differing views and standards into industrial competition upon the same soil.* . . .

Our country should by law, to take effect after the expiration of existing treaties, prevent the immigration into this country of all peoples other than those of the white race, except under restricted conditions relating to international commerce, travel, and education. . . . Japan cannot justly take offense at such action. She would be the first to take such action against the white race were it necessary to maintain her institutions. She is at liberty to pursue the same course. . . . *Thus, upon the expiration of the present treaty with Japan and without attendant attacks upon Japanese sensibilities, public opinion will be so shaped as to force a calm and rational solution of the question by purely domestic and national legislation.*

The conclusion of the whole matter then is that exclusion is the only alternative of race degeneracy or race war.

ORIENTAL vs. AMERICAN LABOR

By A. E. YOELL,

Secretary Asiatic Exclusion League of North America, San Francisco, Cal.

For a proper comprehension of the dangers threatening the wage earning classes in California through the competition of Asiatics it is necessary to take a view of the conditions prevailing in Hawaii, brought about by the predominance of the Asiatic element in the population of that territory. With a population of 170,000 of all races, there are 72,000 Japanese, 25,000 Chinese and about 8,000 Koreans, making the Asiatic element 61 per cent of the whole.

The orientalization of the Hawaiian Islands and the resulting character of the working population by the elimination of white mechanics and laborers have created an acute labor problem, and the white laborer of California fears that the presence of large numbers of Asiatics in that state will bring about conditions similar to those existing in Hawaii. For the wage earner and small merchant, the problem is one of survival in the face of an increasing, irresistible and disastrous competition.

Less than 50 per cent of these Asiatics are engaged in plantation work, and other agricultural pursuits; the remainder are in domestic service, trade and transportation, manufacturing and mechanical pursuits. In some of these lines Asiatic competition is of early date, but during the past five or six years every trade has been invaded, in some instances to the absolute exclusion of the Caucasian element. There are practically no white wage earners engaged in making men's and women's garments and shoes, though a few earn a precarious living by repairing and cobbling. The Japanese are strong competitors in the plumbing trade, and in some places have practically monopolized the work of making tinware for plantation stores, and for sale among working people. The whites are being driven from all the miscellaneous trades very rapidly.

The building trades have also been aggressively invaded by the Japanese, and white mechanics are steadily giving up and forming a procession back to the coast. A white contractor, who used white and Hawaiian labor only, recently said that he had not had a contract of any importance for nearly a year and a half, because he had been ruinously underbid, either by Japanese contractors or white contractors using Asiatic labor exclusively. He called attention to a large building being constructed, upon which thirty-five workmen were employed, and although there were plenty of whites and Hawaiians idle, not a single workman was found on the building except Asiatics. Every detail of the building—carpentering, plastering, plumbing, painting—was done by Asiatic labor. The only city occupations not yet subject to keen Japanese competition are the English printing trades and some forms of machinery and metal working.

There is an aspect of the Japanese question in Hawaii which also affects the planters, and it arises out of the preponderance among the laborers of a single nationality, which, to a certain extent, takes out of the hands of owners the control of administration. The Japanese have learned their power and use it unmercifully. Evidence, both direct and indirect, presented itself in 1905, showing that plantation owners fear the power of their Japanese laborers, and endeavor to placate them by concessions not dictated primarily by regard for efficient service. At this writing, June 1, 1909, some 10,000 Japanese plantation laborers are on strike for higher wages, and though the planters are, to some extent, filling their places with the labor available, it may safely be predicted that, as half of the sugar crop remains unmilled, the Japanese will win the day.

The wages paid Orientals in Hawaii on the plantations is about one-third of that paid to whites for the same class of employment. In the miscellaneous trades in Honolulu the difference is not so great, being about 50 per cent, but it is in the mechanical and building trades that the keenest competition by means of reduced wages is felt.

Average Wages Per Day.

	American.	Japanese
Carpenters	$3.99	$2.54
Foreman Carpenters	5.75	2.43
Engineers	4.72	1.66
Foreman Painters	4.00	2.50
Painters	3.25	1.50
Sheet Metal Workers	3.16	1.50
Tinsmiths	3.50	1.50

The foregoing table should be convincing evidence that Americans cannot compete with Asiatics and maintain the present standard of living. That the building trades of California have also been invaded will be seen further on.

In several parts of California conditions prevail closely paralleling those existing in Hawaii, and though the number of Asiatics here is but 89,000,[1] against 105,000 in the islands, the thin edge of the wedge has entered and is being driven home. Mercantile and mechanical pursuits have not, however, been invaded to such an extent as in Hawaii, but the danger is a real one, and will be presented in detail later on.

Wages, Hours of Labor and Conditions in San Francisco

On March 13, 1906, Hon. E. A. Hayes delivered a speech in the House of Representatives, in which he paid particular attention to the competition of Chinese and Japanese in various lines of industry in San Francisco. Since then conditions have grown from bad to worse, until in some lines they have become almost unendurable. The following is compiled from the latest available information:

Seamen: The number of Asiatics sailing between Pacific Coast and trans-Pacific ports is estimated at 3,500, their wages averaging from $5.00 to $7.50 United States gold, against $30.00 paid to the white seamen for similar services. The Pacific Mail Steamship Company, employing Chinese seamen, is virtually being driven out of business by the competition of Japanese liners, and though operating at a considerable yearly loss, is kept in existence through the patriotism of Mr. Harriman, who refuses to haul down the flag from the only line flying the American flag in the Oriental trade.

Butchers: There are employed in the pork trade 200 Chinese, who work sixteen hours per day, against the ten hours of the white butcher. The Chinese handle about 75 per cent of all the pork slaughtered. In consequence of this competition, the white pork butcher has to work for 24 to 50 per cent less wages than those in other branches of the business. Wages,[2]—white butchers, $20 per week; Chinese, $35 per month.

Broom Makers: The Chinese have destroyed competition in this industry by cheap methods and inferior workmanship. The

[1] Japanese, 55,000; Chinese, 30,000; Koreans, 2,000; Hindus, 2,000.
[2] Ruling wages are given in this compilation.

white broom maker works nine hours for $2.50 per day. The Chinese work from ten to fourteen hours for $6.00 to $9.00 per week.

Garment Workers: Including both Chinese and Japanese, there are about 150 establishments employing about 1,000 hands working from ten to twelve hours per day for $4.00 per week on ladies' wear, to $50.00 per month on gentlemen's goods. White workers have a day of nine hours and are paid $9.00 to $20.00 per week, according to the class of goods.

Laundry Workers: There are in San Francisco over 100 Chinese hand-washing laundries and eighteen modern equipped Japanese steam laundries, employing in the aggregate, with Japanese apprentices, about 1,000 hands. These Asiatic laundries are doing at least five-eighths of the laundry work of the city, and the white worker is being constantly reminded by the employer of the difficulty experienced in competing with Mongolians. Before the advent of the Japanese steam laundry (1905) there were 1,650 white union laundry workers; to-day there are only 1,050. The white laundry worker's time is fifty hours per week, wages $6.00 to $18.00 per week. The Japanese time is ten to fourteen hours a day, wages $6.00 to $9.00 per week. The Chinese works as long as he can endure; wages $3.00 to $15.00 per week.

This competition has caused the establishment of Anti-Jap Laundry Leagues throughout the state, and this action has been met by the Japanese by a still further reduction in their price lists, which now stand at about 50 per cent less than that of the white laundries.

Cooks: The number of Asiatics employed varies according to the season. Chinese, 200 to 300; Japanese, 400 to 750. Hours of labor,—white, from 10 to thirteen hours per day; Chinese and Japanese, from fourteen to sixteen hours per day. Wages,—white, $15.00 to $25.00 for six days; Chinese and Japanese, from $25.00 to $35.00 per month, without any day off. The Chinese and Japanese serve meals for ten cents, which entices a certain class of men to extend them their patronage.

In railroad construction throughout the state 200 to 300 Chinese and from 400 to 600 Japanese camp cooks and helpers are employed, the number varying according to the time of the year.

Waiters: The Chinese restaurants, of which there are twenty, employ about 180 of their own countrymen. Of Japanese restaurants there are seventy, in which there are possibly 300 Japanese. In the white restaurants the hours of labor are nine for women, with a wage of $7.00, and ten for men, with a wage of $10.50. The Chinese average thirteen hours for $6.00, and the Japanese fourteen hours for $5.00. In boarding houses and saloons there are probably more than 1,000 Japs employed as cooks, porters and maids-of-all-work, to the exclusion of that number of white workers.

Domestics: In this occupation, that of house servant, the Japanese have supplanted the Chinese, as they have supplanted the white domestic. Mr. Walter V. Stafford, who was state labor commissioner, 1902-1906, declared that 5,000 white girls had been robbed of their employment as domestics by Japanese. This was accomplished by several methods: (1) By the student domestic, who gave his services for board and the privilege of going to school; (2) by the organization of Japanese house-cleaning companies, whose members go out by the hour or day, working between times at shoe repairing and other industries, working at a rate and living under conditions to which no self-respecting white girl can submit. The manager of one of the leading female employment agencies recently said: "Any woman who will pay decent wages and treat her help like human beings can get all the girls needed. People have become so accustomed to Orientals that they forget an American girl cannot live like an Asiatic."

In this connection, it may not be amiss to call attention to a statement made by Mr. Hepburn, of Iowa, in reply to a speech by Mr. Hayes upon the Asiatic question:

They are the choice of all the domestics of the gentleman's own state. I do not hesitate to say that 500,000 could be absorbed into the labor field of the United States and not displace a single American.

The trouble is that there are no Americans to displace because, as has been said before, no self-respecting American girl will enter into competition with Mongolians. It is said by some of our philanthropic publicists in California that the American girl is too hard to please; that she expects too much from her employer; but be that as it may, the following excerpts should be sufficient proof that with all her faults the white girl should be preferred to her Asiatic competitor.[3] Mr. J. D. Putnam, Chinese Inspector at Los Angeles, Cal., says:

Report of United States Industrial Commission, Vol XV, page 799.

Those not acquainted with Chinese and their habits and customs, cannot realize the demoralizing effect they have upon the young and rising generation. I venture to say that more girls are ruined by the wily Chinese, as few of them as there are, comparatively, than all other criminal classes combined. Stop and think of the Chinese at the wash tub with a young girl's wardrobe, then as her chambermaid, with his head shaved and his white apron, and with that bland smile on his face, and then turn and look at the ladies who visit their places. Can you believe that the Chinese are more than human? The Chinese as a class are a born set of bribers, gamblers, polygamists and perjurers, and when anyone will show me one actually converted Chinaman among them, then it will be one I have not met. You may have evening mission schools for young Chinese men for young ladies to teach, and you will have no lack of pupils; but take the ladies away and put young men equally capable and religious in their places, and in a short time you will not have a Chinaman attending school.

If in the above you substitute the word "Japanese" for Chinese, and then underline each word, you will still have but a faint conception of the conditions with which the American girl has to compete if she wishes to earn a living by domestic service.

Building Trades: For the purpose of securing information concerning the inroads likely to be made by the Japanese on the building trades, Dr. Carl Saalfield submitted plans, for a house he contemplated building, to Japanese architects and contractors, with the following results: He found that the Japanese have entered into all the thirty-four trades connected with the building of a modern house. He found that they would build a fine house for $2,000 less than the lowest bid from an American firm. That bid was $5,800. The Japanese offered to build it for $3,800. They would do everything, from the excavating to the plumbing, gasfitting, painting and decorating,—turning over the keys for a finished house. The doctor, thinking there had been some mistake, went over the plans with them, even to the tile laying, but they stood by their figures. They pay their carpenters $1.50 per day and their laborers about 60 per cent less than a white laborer receives. The item for common labor has been figured by the white American at $700—the Japanese figured it at $250. In various parts of the state they have done much cement and concrete work, and good work, too, but at a figure which a white man cannot touch and live.

The figures following were compiled from the report of the Twelfth Census, 1900, and while we cannot go behind them, we are convinced, through reports emanating from the Treasury Department officials, that a large number of Mongolians, both Chinese and Japanese, succeeded in evading the enumerators. Keeping that statement in mind, the following should certainly be of interest:

MONGOLIANS ENGAGED IN THE BUILDING INDUSTRIES, 1900.

Occupation,	Chinese.	Japanese.	Total.
Carpenters	417	666	1,083
Masons (brick and stone)	4	49	53
Painters and Varnishers	105	56	161
Plasterers	...	4	4
Plumbers and Gas Fitters	...	1	1
Marble and Stone Cutters	...	33	33
Tin Plate Workers	116	12	128
Cabinet Makers	16	7	23
Saw and Planing Mill Workers	76	165	241
	734	993	1,727

It is thus seen that there were 734 Chinese and 993 Japanese building mechanics in 1900, but how many of them were in California we have no means of finding out. We do know, however, that since 1900 over 50,000 Japanese have come to the mainland of the United States from the Territory of Hawaii, and that the Japanese population of California has increased over 600 per cent; and it would be the height of folly to assume that there was not more than a fair sprinkling of building mechanics among them. We know further that during the years 1901 to 1907, both inclusive, 109,406 Japanese entered the United States through legal channels, and of that number 4,446 were skilled mechanics. It is not reasonable to believe that they will be content to work as field laborers and domestics when the opportunity is afforded them to invade the building industries.

Farm Labor: The employment of Japanese upon the farms of California is a measure which, though apparently necessary at one time, is now a source of regret to those responsible for their introduction.

In 1895 a labor contractor in Honolulu offered to place 30,000 Japanese laborers in the agricultural districts of California, who would work for $12.00 per month and board themselves. This proposition was taken up with avidity by the farmers, who were always short of help in the harvest season, and the records of the steamship companies show that many thousands came. In a very short while the white farm laborers were driven to the large cities, and the Japanese had the field of agriculture to themselves. It was not long before the farmers discovered that they had created a "Frankenstein." Instead of having "cheap" labor, they soon had to pay the Japanese more wages than they formerly paid the white workingmen. By working in gangs under a head man, and by combination through the various Japanese associations, they have advanced their wages to $2.00 a day and upward. In many cases, the farmer becoming discouraged by the continual raids upon his pocket, leased his ranch to Japanese on shares, to be again outwitted by his Oriental "friends." The last resort was to lease or sell outright, until the Japanese own and lease in the aggregate some 150,000 acres of the most fertile land in the state. The result is that to-day the potato crop of the state is controlled by George Shima, the "Potato King," who compels us to pay five cents per pound for potatoes at retail.

In Southern California the celery crop and other vegetables are controlled by Japanese, the white growers being helpless against them. In the Santa Clara Valley, one of the most beautiful parts of the state, the berry crop is almost entirely in the hands of the Japanese.

Recently, however, the Farmers' Educational and Co-operative Society has taken the matter in hand, and is seeking the co-operation of organized labor to aid in marketing farm products raised and packed entirely by white labor. The following excerpts from the Twelfth Biennial Report of the California Bureau of Labor Statistics illustrates in a vivid manner the conditions existing in several of the districts dominated by the Japanese:

Watsonville.—Men of standing in the community who employ Japanese and have no race prejudice, apparently, and who are distinctly opposed to labor unions, largely on account of the opposition of the latter to Orientals, declare the Japanese dishonest and inferior in this regard to the Chinese. When the Japanese arrived in the Pajaro Valley they were welcomed by the merchants; to-day the merchants bitterly complain that the Japanese have become their very close competitors. They run restaurants, barbershops and ready-made clothing stores in the City of Watsonville and operate busses and delivery wagons in the adjacent territory. One bank positively refuses to open any account with the Japanese because of their absolute dishonesty, the same bank welcoming business from the Chinese. The local postmaster places the Jap in a class by himself, and will not cash his money orders without other evidence than the possession of the order, and there is a large postoffice money order business with the Japanese on account of the fact that certain banks decline to do business with them.

Vacaville.—The Japanese came to Vaca Valley, Solano County, about eighteen years ago and commenced working for very small wages. Their number increased until they not only displaced about all the white labor, but almost entirely ran out the Chinese. They then began to rent orchards, paying cash in advance, thereby undermining the Chinese, who generally paid with a share of the crops. The Jap outbid the Chinaman until he ceased to be a factor. This condition developed until the Japanese control, by lease and ownership, half of the fruit farms in the valley at this time.

Latterly their handling of leased ranches has been less satisfactory. They cultivate indifferently, or for immediate results, to the serious detriment of the property. Prior to the advent of the Japanese, Vaca Valley was renowned for its orchards, which attracted wide attention, especially on account of the superior methods of pruning and cultivating. To-day there can be no boasting in this respect. Large shipping firms give the Japanese credit and backing, and aid them in obtaining leases, etc., on account of their ability to obtain labor in the fruit season. The white rancher can scarcely obtain such aid, on account of his lack of assurance of sufficient help. In other words, the Japanese have the best organization.

It is generally conceded that 90 per cent of all the people met, walking or driving on all the country roads around Vacaville, are Japanese. One of the prominent fruit growers and shippers in the valley estimates the fruit orchards of Vaca Valley and adjoining foothills at 15,000 acres, more than half of which are in the hands of Japanese lessees, or owners, principally leased. He declared the Jap is an expert at drawing all the vitality out of the land and the trees. Land values have shrunk one-third in the past fifteen years.

The Japanese stores, of which there are six in Vacaville, are doing more than 50 per cent of the general merchandise business of the town, and 90 per cent of the farm supply business.

Fresno.—In Fresno, as at other points, it is generally conceded that the Jap is merciless when he has his employer at a disadvantage; that he will work cheaply until all competition is eliminated, and then strike for higher wages, totally disregarding any agreement or contract.

There is no place in the state where the problem is so grave, from the fact that the raisin territory (and Fresno is the greatest producer of raisins on the planet) depends almost entirely on the Orientals. Last year over 4,000 cars of raisins were shipped from Fresno. The more intelligent citizens realize the gravity of the situation both from the economic and racial sides. Similar conditions in a lesser degree exist in the different berry and sugar beet sections of the state. The general persistency with which the Japanese are breaking into many industries, their frugality, their ambition and their lack of business morality, render them more formidable than the Chinese.

It is astonishing that in the light of this evidence so many public men, in and out of Congress, declare that the labor necessities of the Pacific Coast demand the presence of these Asiatics. They say that our fruit orchards, mines and seed farms cannot be worked without them. It were better that they never be developed than that our white laborers be degraded and driven from the soil. The same arguments were used a century and more ago, to justify the importation of African labor. I assert, most emphatically, that there is no demand for labor on the Pacific Coast that cannot be fully met with white laborers if conditions are made such that they will wish to come and remain here. As it is now, no self-respecting white laborer will work beside the Mongolian upon any terms. The proposition, whether we shall have white or yellow labor on the Pacific Coast, must soon be settled, for we cannot have both. If the Mongolian is permitted to occupy the land, the white laborer from east of the Rockies will not come here—he will shun California as he would a pestilence. And who can blame him?

NOTE.—The authorities consulted for this paper were:

Hawaii: Third Report on Hawaii, published as Bulletin 66 of U. S. Bureau of Labor, September, 1906.

California: Reports of California, Bureau of Labor Statistics, 1898-1908.

Report of U. S. Industrial Commission, Vol. XV.

Correspondence of County Officials of California and the voluminous files of the Asiatic Exclusion League of San Francisco.

MISUNDERSTANDING OF EASTERN AND WESTERN STATES REGARDING ORIENTAL IMMIGRATION

By Hon. Albert G. Burnett,

Associate Justice, District Court of Appeals of California, Third Appellate District, Sacramento, Cal.

The people who for sixty years have been building for themselves homes on the Pacific slope have in their veins, as have their kin in the East from whom they parted, the blood of the Puritan and the Cavalier, intermingled by the infusion from European countries. The short space of time during which they have lived apart and the few miles which separate them from each other have not caused them to become strangers. The pioneers of the West carried thither, and their descendants have inherited, the traditions, the laws, the customs, the ideals of their ancestors on the Atlantic. If, then, there is a difference of opinion or a misunderstanding between the people of the East and those of the West on the subject of Oriental immigration to the United States, it must be due solely to environment.

The people of the New England and Middle States have for more than half a century been accustomed to seeing the great flood of European immigrants pouring through their gates. While notes of warning have frequently been uttered against this invasion, the people at large have noticed that in the second or third generation the newcomers have generally become assimilated with our own population and in the main the country has benefited by their coming. The easterners have not, as yet, faced the problem of an influx of aliens unassimilable with ourselves.

But on the shores of the Pacific the white man, at first curiously noticing the incoming advance-guard of the Asiatic races, soon took genuine alarm at the thought that untold millions of these people might domicile themselves with us, introducing to our people dangerous forms of vice and creating a labor situation which it was feared would banish the white laborer from the coast; and it was also perceived that this vast exodus of coolies would not appreciably diminish the supply in the over-populated Orient. It was comparatively easy to stem the tide when it was the Chinese who were coming; the problem now is, in many respects, an entirely different one. While we are grappling with the question of the influx of Japanese and are uncertain as to the final outcome—or, at least, as to the method of achieving the only solution which will be conceded on the coast—we are threatened with an invasion of England's half-starved, superstitious, caste-bound Hindus, whose evil propensities in certain directions seemed delightfully interesting fiction coming from the fascinating pen of Kipling, but are now discovered to be none too truthfully portrayed by him. The West *is* alarmed.

The antipathy existing in the states beyond the Rocky Mountains to the natives of Nippon is due partly to racial, partly to economic causes. While the few may dream of the coming Utopia . where the "Brotherhood of Man" has become an assured fact, the masses in every nation are still governed largely by inherited prejudices, and of all these race prejudice is, perhaps, the strongest. When an occasional marriage of a white woman to a Japanese raises a storm of protest among the white people of the community, it is no greater than that raised by the Japanese themselves, and for the same reason; each race is opposed to the intermarriage because it thinks its own member is degrading himself or herself by becoming a party to it.

There exists no prouder or more sensitive race than the Japanese, and to this fact is due, in great degree, the difficulty of dealing with the situation. The methods pursued in the exclusion of the Chinese, if followed in the case of their island neighbors, would undoubtedly lead to serious trouble, if not to open hostilities. Despite certain warlike utterances in some of the western newspapers, the great majority of the people on the Pacific Coast are fully alive to the horrors of war and do not wish recklessly to provoke one with any nation.

Again, the experience of the southern states in dealing with an alien race, even though domiciled there for centuries, has served as a vivid warning to the people of the West to avoid the perplexing questions which have for so long harassed the South. They believe that one such race problem should be sufficient to cause us to forever guard against the introduction of another.

The economic questions involved in the employment of Japanese labor are complex, and there is no unanimity of opinion on this subject among the people of the Pacific states. There are two prominent interests desiring more or less freedom of entry for the Asiatic races—the steamship companies and the horticulturist and farmer. The reasons actuating the former are obvious and need not be adverted to. But the question of labor in the orchards and vineyards and on the farms is of vital interest to the men by whose efforts there are produced annually in California alone fruit crops valued at thirty millions of dollars. On account of climatic and other conditions, many white men are averse to performing certain portions of the farm and orchard work. In many cases where they have been employed, there has been a tendency among them to quit their employment when the first pay-day arrived and to find con-genial company in the saloons of the nearest town. It is not a question of low wages altogether, for Japanese frequently earn from three to five dollars per day in the harvest season. The crying need of the orchardist and farmer is reliable labor, and it is claimed that the only laborer who has yet come up to the requirements is the Chinese. He is as a general rule patient, reliable and uncomplaining, and will faithfully perform any contract he may enter into even at a pecuniary loss to himself, but he is barred by the exclusion act. The Japanese laborer is not as honest as the Chinese. He has no scruples about violating a contract with his white employer when he sees that by so doing he can place the owner at such disadvantage that, in order to save his crop, he will submit to demands that are extortionate. Nor is the Japanese content to remain an employee, but by cunning and trickery he forces the white land owner either to lease or sell to him his land. A favorite method of dealing with a white lessor is so to prune his orchard that in two or three years it will produce no revenue, and the discouraged owner will sell for any price.

The fruit-growers of California, in convention assembled, have officially memorialized Congress demanding that the Chinese exclusion law be modified and that a fixed and liberal number of Chinese and an equal number of Japanese be permitted admission annually. Their claim is that it is practically impossible to secure white men to perform certain work necessary in the orchards and on the farms —the primary processes, so-called—and that Asiatic labor in that particular is, therefore, non-competitive.

Opposed to the comparatively few who can profitably utilize the labor of the Orient are the white workingmen, who believe that the presence of large numbers of Japanese and Chinese laborers will tend to a reduction in wages and a lowering of the general standard of living. The leaders of union labor are particularly active in denunciation of Asiatic immigration. To the student of labor conditions on the Pacific Coast, it seems undeniable that the unrestricted entry of Japanese laborers would eventually destroy the home of the American workingman. They live together thickly in violation of all sanitary rules, and where they settle in numbers the American is forced to vacate. If he would, the white man could not live as do these aliens. Nor do the immigrants remain in the country districts, engaged in farm work; large sections of cities and towns are occupied by them and in many branches of labor they are in direct competition with the whites.

For the above and many other reasons there is rapidly crystalizing a sentiment, not only in the western part of the United States, but to an even more intense degree in British Columbia, that this portion of North America must remain "a white man's country." Californians are at present content to accept the assurances from Washington that this end can be attained by diplomacy. In the meantime the state government is taking steps to ascertain how many Japanese there are within its borders and whether they have ceased coming, as has been stated more than once.

There has been in the eastern states a very great misconception of the position of California with reference to the admission of Japanese to the public schools. Many of the hostile criticisms in the newspapers are predicated upon the assumption that the benefits of education were being denied children of Japanese parentage. This is erroneous. Boys born in America of Asiatic parents will eventually become voters, and California realizes, as fully as do any of its sister states, the necessity of having an intelligent, educated electorate. It is desirous of giving to them the same education that it does to white children. But the people of the state do object seriously to "Japanese school-boys" of eighteen years and upward attending the primary and intermediate grades and studying with white children many years their juniors. The Japanese code of morals is constructed on an entirely different principle from ours. The radical difference in the standards of morality may be illustrated by reference to the case of a Japanese boy who was criminally prosecuted last year for sending through the mails to a white girl schoolmate an objectionable letter. While such matters may be entirely proper in Japan, California does not intend to tolerate them, nor would any other state in the Union do so.

For many years the city of San Francisco has maintained a separate school for the instruction of Chinese children, with white teachers and the same course of study as in other schools of the city. Chinese parents have made no protest, but have generally agreed that separate schools are preferable. But when a proposition is made to have Japanese attend so-called Oriental schools a storm is raised which causes extreme agitation in Tokyo and in Washington and column upon column of denunciation in the press of both countries.

California claims that the government of its public schools is a subject purely within state control; that the federal government has no power to exercise any supervision over the matter; and the state proposes to regulate the schools so as to confer the greatest good upon the greatest number. There is no desire, except upon the part of a very few persons, to stir up race hatred. On the contrary, it is believed that separate schools would assist very materially in arriving at an intelligent solution of the problems involved, by removing one very serious cause of irritation.

The West is not unduly or at all excited over the question of immigration from Japan; it is only determined. It has heard from Washington that the Mikado's government is going to refuse permission to its subjects to come to the United States. It hopes this will be done, but it is somewhat dubious when it hears rumors from day to day of the vast numbers of Japanese who are debarking in British Columbia and stealing their way across the border. If the influx cannot be stopped in one way it can in some other, and the West is insistent in the demand that it be done by some means, and soon. The Pacific states comprise an empire of vast potentialities and capable of supporting a population of many millions. Those now living there propose that it shall continue to be a home for them and their children, and that they shall not be overwhelmed and driven eastward by an ever-increasing yellow and brown flood.

THE JAPANESE PROBLEM IN CALIFORNIA

By Sidney G. P. Coryn,
Of "The Argonaut," San Francisco, Cal.

The object of the present paper is rather to state a problem than either to suggest a remedy or to assume the position of arbitrator between the conflicting interests. For many years the Japanese have been an irritation in California. For many years the newspapers of the state—and notably the San Francisco "Chronicle," a journal of responsible conservatism—have drawn attention to the increasing numbers of Japanese immigrants and the consequent injury to the interests of the country. Some five years ago these complaints came energetically to a head. Statistics were compiled from the scanty material at command, opinions were collected, and grievances stated, with the result that the Japanese question became an issue of magnitude.

California had already passed through a race agitation against the Chinese that at one time threatened a formidable convulsion. Was she upon the high road to another and a more dangerous protest against a people flushed with the successes of a great war and in no mood to tolerate adverse discrimination? The gravity of the issue made it difficult to halt between two opinions. The last legislature was nearly equally divided between the anti-Japanese who wished to impose various restrictions upon the Asiatics, and those who may not have been pro-Japanese but who were at least unwilling to do anything that might embarrass the federal government. The governor of the state and the speaker of the assembly threw their weight against the proposed legislation. Even the anti-Japanese press admitted that the time was inopportune for restrictions, and so the agitation temporarily subsided. That it will be renewed there cannot be the slightest doubt.

The discussion served many good ends. It gave cohesion and a voice to the interests that believed themselves to be specifically threatened by the Japanese invasion. It brought to the front also those other interests that held themselves to be directly benefited. It had the effect of arousing the serious interest of the Japanese government and persuading it to energetic measures for the abatement of a nuisance dangerous to itself. The activities of the great immigration companies of Japan were discouraged and a system of passports was imposed upon the emigrating classes. Whether as a result of these measures or from other causes, it is certain that the incoming stream has been substantially lessened,—we shall presently see to what extent.

That there are classes who favor as well as disfavor the Japanese is an important point, and we have no right to assume selfish or unsocial motives either in one case or the other. If it can be urged against the labor unionist of San Francisco that he keeps exclusively in view his own wage scale and his class domination, so in the same way can the fruit grower be charged with an indifference to the well-being of the community at large so long as he can always find a sufficiency of underpaid Asiatics to do his work and to save him the expense of sanitation and of hygienic conditions. It is better to avoid the assumption of sinister motives.

San Francisco has had to stand the brunt of the Asiatic invasion and her voice is naturally the loudest. In many instances we need no deep research to see that the complaints are well founded. Japanese shoe repairing shops, for instance, are to be found dotted all over the city. Japanese laundries are nearly as numerous. There are hundreds of Japanese janitors, and Japanese house cleaners, while the invasion of other branches of activity is steady and persistent. Divisions of the city are becoming known as Japanese quarters; and Japanese stores in a chronic state of "selling off" are to be found everywhere. All these things mean the dispossession of white men. The Japanese shoe repairing shops are said without contradiction to be controlled and financed by a capitalist of Tokyo, who requires that each of his beneficiaries shall take an apprentice who will in due time start his own shop with his own apprentice. And all these things mean not merely competition, but underselling. The Japanese will enter into no trade agreement, he will respect no standard of prices. He is a law unto himself, and his only rule is to get the business at any and every cost. It is not surprising that the opinion among the wage earners of San Francisco is nearly unanimous. The presence of the Japanese trader means that the white man must either go out of busines or abandon his standard of comfort and sink to the level of the Asiatic, who will sleep under his counter and subsist upon food that would mean starvation to his white rival.

A glance at statistics, so far as they are available, will help us to understand the situation and to measure the danger. Conservative estimates of the number of Japanese now in California vary from 45,000 to 50,000. The general census report of 1900 gives the number at 10,151. The records show that the Japanese landed from foreign ports from October, 1899, to September, 1904, numbered 10,524. During 1903 and 1904 7,270 Japanese arrived from Hawaii, but there are no figures for Hawaiian arrivals for the two years ending December 31, 1903. During 1904 Japanese to the number of 672 arrived from Victoria, but there is no record from this source for the previous three years. For the two years ending September 30, 1906, the net increase of arrivals over departures at San Francisco was 13,658, and for the subsequent two years the increase was 1,213. These sadly incomplete figures represent a total of 43,488. Even were they complete there would still be no inclusion of the Japanese who enter unregistered or surreptitiously from Canada and from Mexico. They are certainly numerous.

The distribution of these people affords an explanation of the louder complaints emanating from San Francisco. Assuming the total to be 45,000—certainly underestimated—we find 12,000 in San Francisco, 6,000 in Los Angeles, 9,000 in the vicinities of Sacramento and Fresno, and 18,000 in all other parts of the state.

The year 1908 witnessed a marked decrease in the Japanese population, due partly to the numbers who returned to their own country and partly to the efforts of the Japanese government to restrict emigration. From October 1, 1906, to October 1, 1907, the net increase was 3,719, while from October 1, 1907, to October 1, 1908, we have a decrease of 2,506, the net result for the two years being an increase of only 1,213.

While opinion in San Francisco is nearly unanimous as to the undesirability of the Japanese as residents and traders, it must be admitted that there is by no means such unanimity among the fruit growers of the country districts. Labor is always hard to obtain upon the fruit ranch, and the Asiatic is frequently welcomed as an alternative to a partial loss of the fruit crop. The Bureau of Labor statistics furnish us with the opinions of 132 farmers upon the advantages of Japanese labor. Nearly all of them employ Asiatics, but while some of them do so willingly the majority seem to make a virtue of necessity. Here are some half-dozen quotations from the reports, taken almost at random:

> Whites, we regret to say, are the least dependable, and Japanese are only half as good as Chinese.
>
> I find that the Japanese as a rule take care of their money and work steadier than the white laborer.
>
> They (Asiatics) are very poor help to employ by the day or month.
>
> I do not employ any Japanese. You cannot depend on them.
>
> I have no use for Japanese. I like the Chinese better. You cannot depend on the Japanese: they will strike when you are busy and a contract with them don't amount to anything.
>
> I have employed both the Chinese and Japanese on my ranch, and find that I like the Chinese the better, for if you are exceedingly rushed a Chinaman will not strike for higher wages and leave you in the lurch, as the Jap surely does.
>
> I am opposed to the exclusion of the Japanese. We would be in a bad fix without their help. I prefer them to the kind of white men who apply for work.

Wherever we find comparisons between the Japanese and the Chinese it is always to the disadvantage of the former. A common practice is to rent the fruit orchard to the Japanese or to sell to them the standing crop, leaving all the responsibilities of harvest and market to the purchaser. Opinions as to the morality and reliability of the Japanese are nearly always adverse. Many of the reports complain that the Japanese never loses an accidental advantage, and never allows contract or promise to stand in the way of attainment. The need of the white man is the opportunity for the Japanese, and he never fails to take it.

It may be supposed that the 132 farmers who furnished their opinions to the Bureau of Labor are too few in number to form a basis for an adequate estimate of the general sentiment. That fact was doubtless taken into consideration by the last California legislature when it ordered the preparation of a census of all the Japanese in the state and the collection of information concerning them. These instructions are now being carried out and in the fullest way. Within a few months we shall have not only adequate statistics, but a very large mass of information upon well nigh every point of interest. We shall know how many Japanese are employed, the reasons for their engagement, the nature of the labor that they displaced, how they are paid, lodged, and fed, their progress in social usages, their effectiveness, tractability, sobriety, and reliability. It is upon these returns that the action of the next legislature will be based, and it is certain that action of some kind will be proposed and vigorously sustained, although a continuance of the present decrease in the number of arrivals can hardly fail to have a modifying influence.

A word as to the school situation may not be amiss, for there can be no doubt that the effort to exclude Japanese pupils from the public schools has done more to wound Oriental susceptibilities than anything else. Moreover it has been effectively used in the East to show that the action of California was oppressive and unreasonable. It may be said at once that the Japanese children are well behaved and that there has been no criticism of their deportment, intelligence, or behavior. Indeed it is probably true that if all the Japanese pupils in the common schools had been bona-fide children there would be no complaint registered against them and we should never have heard of the schools question. But a great many of the Japanese pupils are not children in any sense of the word. They are grown men whose status in the schools depends of course upon their knowledge and not upon their age. The Japanese boy of eighteen or twenty years of age who can neither read nor write English must necessarily be assigned to the lower grades and placed in association with white children of a tender age. That fully grown boys, whether Japanese or not, should be placed in daily contact with girls many years younger than themselves is obviously undesirable. In the case of Asiatics it is felt to be still more undesirable, and this without any reflection upon the morals of the Asiatic, but with a recognition that his point of view is radically different. The white parent is unwilling that his little girl shall associate upon terms of comradely intimacy with a boy who may presently welcome from Japan the wife whom he has wedded through the kindly mediation of a photograph.

From such considerations, and not merely from a racial spleen, arose the first protests against the Japanese in the public schools. Popular ignorance helped of course to swell the chorus, and industrial jealousies played their accustomed part, but it is hardly surprising that the parents of San Francisco and of California in general should feel their primal rights to be infringed when they are told that they are not at liberty to invoke legislation for the protection of their own children in the schools that they themselves support at enormous cost. With the lack of such a power the principle of self-government would seem to have no meaning.

Up to the present time we have looked mainly at those classes of the community that are brought into direct contact with the Japanese, either suffering from their competition, or availing themselves, willingly or unwillingly, of their aid. But there is another class of the community whose opinions, more slowly aroused and perhaps less noisily expressed, must ultimately prevail. I mean that class whose training and environment enable them to take a comprehensive survey of the situation and to reach conclusions but little dependent upon the economic stresses of the moment. From this class come certain considerations worthy of grave attention.

According to the terms of the present laws of the United States Constitution the Japanese cannot be naturalized. They cannot become American citizens. An amalgamation, entirely foreign as it is to their own ambitions and perhaps to their potentialities, is expressly barred by the fundamental law of this country. It will be seen at once that a portentous situation is created by the presence in our midst of a large and increasing body of aliens of marked intelligence and ambition, who will not and can not merge with their environment, and whose natural clannishness serves still further to accentuate a dividing line traced alike by law, by nature, and by inclination. Is there not good reason to fear that a demarcation already marked by antipathy and by jealousy may speedily become one of hostility, and that we may even create an *imperium in imperio* dangerous to ourselves and fruitful of discord and dissension?

It is hard to determine what the status of such a caste must become. The precedent of the Chinese now in California does not help us at all. The Chinese exclusion law is rigidly enforced and the number of Chinese is decreasing, but it must be remembered that the Chinese temperament is wholly unlike that of the Japanese. The Chinaman dreads competition with the white man, and avoids it; the Japanese courts it. The Chinaman is entirely content to do those kinds of labor that the white man shrinks from; the Japanese wishes to meet the white man on his own ground, and to oust him from it. The Chinaman is willing to be a hewer of wood and a drawer of water; the Japanese has no aptitude for menial tasks nor any intention of performing them except as stepping stones to his own high ambitions.

The Japanese in California must be either a successful competitor with the white man, or must be beaten in such competition by a lowering of the white man's standard of living, or he must be placed in a menial caste and kept there. Which choice is the greater evil? From the first two we shrink as we would from ruin. The third is perhaps the most insidious evil of them all and the most corrupting, and it is one moreover from which the Japanese himself will save us by his own ambitions. No community can remain free if it tolerates a clearly marked menial caste, if it allows the existence of such a caste to place a stigma upon any form of honorable labor. Already we see the marks of that stain upon the industries that the Asiatic has made his own. Already we see something like a "poor white" caste in the orchards and fruit fields of the state.

The Japanese problem is a thorny one. It will be solved not by popular clamor but by clear-headed statesmanship, and upon a basis of recognition that a moral principle is here involved and that our standard of right must be the ultimate benefit of the social organization that is our own.

A WESTERN VIEW OF THE RACE QUESTION

By Hon. Francis G. Newlands,
United States Senator from Nevada.

It is apparent that a change is necessary in our methods of dealing with the problem of undesirable immigration and the occasional disturbances growing out of it. The characteristic inertia of a great mass of people, naturally optimistic and easy-going, is nowhere more strikingly manifested than in their treatment of what is really one of the most vital and far-reaching problems with which we have to deal. If there is one question more than any other which requires the elimination of every consideration of opportunism, it is the one which involves the strains of blood that are to mingle in our descendants' veins, the competition which our laboring men must meet, and the maintenance of our high standard of comfort and social efficiency. Viewed in this light it is to be regretted that wise anticipatory action, of a character which might prevent the occasional outbreaks of race prejudice recently presenting such difficulties, has not been taken.

The race question is the most important one now confronting the nation. As to the black race we have already drifted into a condition which seriously suggests the limitation of the political rights heretofore, perhaps mistakenly, granted them, the inauguration of a humane national policy which, by co-operative action by the nation and the southern states, shall recognize that the blacks are a race of children, requiring guidance, industrial training, and the development of self-control, and other measures designed to reduce the danger of that race complication, formerly sectional, but now rapidly becoming national.

But as a resident of the Pacific Coast region, the problem of Asiatic immigration comes nearer home, and it is upon that subject that I will say a few words. Entertaining no prejudice against any foreign race, and particularly admiring the vigor, courage, and patriotism of the people of Japan, and disposed to advance rather than to thwart her career of national greatness, we of the West are yet profoundly impressed with the view that the United States, possessing a vast territory as yet undeveloped and capable of supporting many times its present population, with natural resources unrivaled anywhere, with climates adapted to every people, will, with the cheapening of transportation, draw to itself the surplus population of all nations. Nature has classified the peoples of the world mainly under four colors: the white, the black, the yellow and the brown. Confronting us on the east lies Europe, with a total poulation of about 300,000,000 white people. We are finding it difficult to assimilate even the immigrants of the white race from that continent, and have been obliged to restrict such immigration.

Confronting our Pacific Coast lies Asia, with nearly a billion people of the yellow and brown races, who, if there were no restrictions, would quickly settle upon and take possession of our entire western coast and intermountain region.

History teaches that it is impossible to make a homogeneous people by the juxtaposition upon the same soil of races differing in color. Race tolerance, under such conditions, means race amalgamation, and this is undesirable. Race intolerance means, ultimately, race war and mutual destruction or the reduction of one race to servitude. The admission of a race of a different color, in a condition of servitude, is foreign to the spirit of our institutions, which demands equal rights to all within our jurisdiction.

The competition of such a race would involve industrial disturbance and hostility, requiring the use of a large armed force to maintain peace and order, with the probability that the nation representing the race thus protected would never be satisfied that the means employed were adequate. The presence of the Chinese, who are patient and submissive, would not create as many complications as the presence of the Japanese, whose strong and virile qualities would constitute an additional element of difficulty. Our friendship with Japan, therefore, for whose territorial and race integrity the American people have been in active sympathy in all her struggles, demands that this friendship be not put to the test by bringing two such powerful races, of such differing views and standards, into industrial competition upon the same soil.

This can be prevented either by international treaty or by national laws regulating, restricting, or even preventing immigration. International negotiation and treaty is, in my judgment, an unsatisfactory method. It requires a nation with which we have treaty relations to prevent its own people from going where they will—a restriction which we would never apply to our own people in any treaty. We would, therefore, be asking another nation to put a restriction upon the movements of its people which we would refuse to prescribe regarding our own. There is but one consistent position to assume, and that is, to relegate the whole question to domestic legislation in each country, permitting each to make such regulation, restriction, or prevention of immigration as it sees fit.

Japan cannot justly take offense at such restrictive domestic legislation upon our part. She would be the first to take such action against the white race, were it necessary to do so in order to maintain the integrity of her race and her institutions. She is at liberty to pursue a similar course. Such action constitutes no implication of inferiority of the race excluded; it may even be a confession of inferiority by the excluding race, in its ability to cope economically with the race excluded. It involves neither insult nor the possibility of war, for Japan could not possibly sustain a war, even were her finances in better condition than they are, without the sympathy of the world as to the justness of her cause.

I am opposed to sporadic legislation, here and there, by the various states, intended to meet only local phases of what really constitutes a national peril, phases which will necessarily have to be covered by broad national legislation. I am opposed to terms of opprobrium and of insult. Japan deserves from us only respect and admiration, and we deserve from her a proper regard for the integrity of our race and institutions. The time has come, in my judgment, when the United States, as a matter of self-protection and self-preservation, must declare by statutory enactment that it will not tolerate further race complications upon our soil. Our country, by law to take effect upon the expiration of existing treaties, should prevent the immigration of all peoples other than those of the white race, except under restricted conditions relating to international commerce, travel, and education. It should start immediately upon the serious consideration of a national policy regarding the people of the black race now within our boundaries, which, with a proper regard for humanity, will minimize the danger which they constitute to our institutions and our civilization.

PART TWO

The Argument Against Oriental Exclusion

UN-AMERICAN CHARACTER OF RACE LEGISLATION
BY MAX J. KOHLER, A.M., LL.B.,
FORMERLY ASSISTANT UNITED STATES DISTRICT ATTORNEY, NEW YORK

REASONS FOR ENCOURAGING JAPANESE IMMIGRATION
BY JOHN P. IRISH,
NAVAL OFFICER OF CUSTOMS FOR THE PORT OF SAN FRANCISCO, CAL.

MORAL AND SOCIAL INTERESTS INVOLVED IN RESTRICTING ORIENTAL IMMIGRATION
BY REV. THOMAS L. ELIOT, S.T.D.,
PRESIDENT, BOARD OF TRUSTEES REED INSTITUTE, PORTLAND, ORE.

WHY OREGON HAS NOT HAD AN ORIENTAL PROBLEM
BY F. G. YOUNG,
PROFESSOR OF ECONOMICS AND SOCIOLOGY, UNIVERSITY OF OREGON, EUGENE, ORE.

UN-AMERICAN CHARACTER OF RACE LEGISLATION

By Max J. Kohler, A.M., LL.B.,
Formerly Assistant United States District Attorney, New York.

The above title is designed to express condemnation of legislation discriminating against particular races, and hence the objections to special legislation, commonly called by the ambiguous phrase "class legislation," as far as based on *race distinctions*, will be here considered. Proper classification, and not race discrimination, ought to underlie legislation. As applied to immigration laws, this objection seems to have been first authoritatively formulated by President Roosevelt and his able Secretary of Commerce and Labor, Oscar S. Straus, in official messages presently to be considered, but in principle such legislation is really inconsistent with the fundamental basis on which our government rests.

The war against negro slavery in the United States was conducted upon this same principle. At the Republican National Convention of 1860, before Lincoln was nominated, Joshua R. Giddings moved that the proposed party platform be amended by incorporating therein the preamble of the Declaration of Independence, in order to indicate clearly that the anti-slavery campaign was merely in harmony with that great declaration of human rights and human equality, and after this resolution had failed on account of ultra-conservatism, George William Curtis renewed the motion in slightly modified form, "daring," in the language of his biographer,[1] "the representatives of the party of freedom meeting on the borders of the free prairies in a hall dedicated to the advancemnt of liberty, to reject the doctrine of the Declaration of Independence, affirming the equality and defining the rights of men; the speech fell like a spark upon tinder, and the amendment was adopted with a shout of enthusiasm."

Similarly, Charles Sumner, the father of our "Civil Rights" legislation, constantly invoked the principles of the Declaration of Independence in support of his proposed measures, as also in his

[1] Cary's Curtis, pp. 134-5; compare Carl Schurz's Memorial Address in honor of Curtis, December 7, 1903.

appeal to strike out color distinctions from our naturalization laws, when the negro was being enfranchised, but the Mongolian was still being discriminated against. "It is 'all men,' and not a race or color, that was placed under protection of the Declaration, and such was the voice of our fathers on the 4th of July, 1776," he argued in the United States Senate on July 4, 1870.[2] So, also, in the leading case of Yick Wo *vs.* Hopkins, 118 U. S. 356, the Supreme Court of the United States, with Justice Stanley Matthews as its spokesman, followed the utterances of the fathers of the republic, in reversing a decision of the California Supreme Court, and determined that a San Francisco ordinance was violative of the fourteenth amendment of the federal constitution in providing that it should be unlawful for persons to engage in the laundry business within that city, without having first obtained the consent of the board of supervisors, except the same be located in a building constructed either of brick or stone, under cover of which Chinese laundrymen were forbidden to transact their business, unlike those of other races. Said the court: "The fundamental rights to life, liberty and the pursuit of happiness, considered as individual possessions, are secured by those maxims of constitutional law which are monuments showing the victorious progress of the race in securing to men the blessings of civilization under the reign of just and equal laws, so that, in the famous language of the Massachusetts Bill of Rights, the government of the commonwealth 'may be a government of laws and not of men.' . . . Class legislation, discriminating against some and favoring others, is prohibited, but legislation which in carrying out a public purpose is limited in its application, if within the sphere of its operation it affects all persons similarly situated, is not within the amendment." Even the form of the ordinance, which concealed its ulterior anti-Chinese purpose, was penetrated by the court, in ferreting out its illegal, discriminating character.

Curiously enough, little has been written even upon class legislation in general, much less concerning legislation based upon race discriminations. The agitation against such special legislation, though it has found expression within certain limits in the fourteenth amendment to the federal constitution, in federal statutes and treaties, and in constitutional provisions in various states, for-

[2] See works of Chas. Sumner, Vol. XIII, p. 482. See also XIV, 286, 301; XV, 355.

bidding anything except general legislation, upon various subjects, is, however, comparatively recent in origin, despite such isolated utterances as have been cited. Mr. Bryce, in his "American Commonwealth," writing in 1888, well points out that such prohibitions began to be adopted only during fifteen years preceding that date, approximately, and the fourteenth amendment was of course framed in consequence of our Civil War. The federal "civil rights" acts were passed to carry this amendment into effect, and various states thereafter adopted similar laws themselves. These restraints, such as they are, apply almost exclusively to our state governments merely, and do not affect the federal government or its agencies. Our "Bill of Rights" provisions were aimed at abuses with which the fathers of our republic were familiar, and excessive, unwise, discriminating legislation, was not then prominent among the evils thus to be avoided. In fact, we are all too prone, in these days of never-ceasing legislative activity, to overlook, in the language of Henry Sumner Maine, "how excessively rare in the world was sustained legislative activity till rather more than fifty years ago" (written in 1885), "that the enthusiasm for legislative change took its rise, not in a popularly governed country, not in England, but in France," and was quickened particularly by Rousseau's conception of the "omnipotent democratic state, rooted in natural right, which has at its absolute disposal everything which individual men value, their property, their persons and their independence," and by Bentham's plan of lodging legislative direction in the greatest number of the people, in the expectation that in employing this power in accordance with their will, they will legislate for and effect the greatest happiness of the greatest number.[8]

In fact, with the exception of discriminations against the negro, we had extremely few enactments based upon race distinctions upon our statute books until our Civil War period, and those that existed were nearly all survivals of the common law. Even our "Alien and Sedition Laws," adopted in 1798, largely through fear that we would be embroiled in the intense foreign wars then raging, which were proving so injurious to us and our commerce, were denounced in the Kentucky and Virginia resolutions drafted by such statesmen as Jefferson and Madison, and resulted in large degree in encompassing the ruin of the unpopular party which stood sponsor for

[8]Maine: "Popular Government," 2d ed., p. 127 *et seq.*

them, and did not encourage our chief political parties to attempt further legislation against aliens in general nor individual races in particular, even in the days of "Know-Nothingism."[4] It is in fact true, generally speaking, that our legislative race discriminations have been confined almost entirely to enactments against the negro, against the Chinese, and latterly also against the Japanese. Though to-day our anti-Chinese laws happen to be largely federal in character, the structure of our government, with its checks and balances, has made the federal government the chief bulwark against such discriminatory legislation, thanks to constitutional provisions in the shape of the fourteenth amendment and treaties which under the constitution are the "supreme law of the land." Again and again have federal treaties with foreign governments been successfully invoked, from the beginning of our history on, to override state discriminations against aliens, including such common law disabilities as made an alien incapable of owning land.

The anthropologist tells us that the formation of the tribe or race was a step in the progress of man, and that originally, each tribe or race protected only its own members, and viewed all outside of its fold not merely with suspicion, but with dislike and hatred. In the progress of civilization the laws were recast so as to remove racial discriminations, and to protect all classes. This progress was effected largely through treaties with particular countries, granting their citizens and subjects full rights, until nearly all civilized men became united together by such ties, and race discriminations became rare exceptions. In fact, our own country, above all, has been in the van in combatting race antagonisms. Says Professor Shaler in his extremely suggestive book, "The Neighbor:"[5] "As soon as an ethnic society is organized, it takes on many of the characteristics of the primitive animal individual, it lives for itself alone. Other groups of like nature are its enemies to whom no faith of any kind is owed. To plunder them is not theft, to slay those who are of them is not murder, they are outside of the pale of all obligations whatever. . . . The most significant peculiarity of the American people, that which in my opinion sets them more apart from the rest of the world than any other, is the relative absence

[4] See the interesting summary by John Bach McMaster of "The Riotous Career of the Know-Nothings," in his collection of essays entitled "With the Fathers."
[5] Pp. 42, 43-4.

of the tribe-forming motive among them. While in Europe there is a general tendency to disbelieve in all men, even of the same race, who are not well known—a humor which is least, but still discernible in Great Britain, and increases to the lands about the Mediterranean—in the United States there is hardly more than a trace of this humor and that appears to be steadily lessening. In general, the American is characterized by an almost unreasonable belief in the likeness to himself of the neighbor, however far parted by race, speech or creed. This is so strong that even the Civil War did not shake it; it served rather to affirm the mutual confidence." Even Professor Shaler, however, notes certain exceptions to this tendency, notably in our attitude towards the negro, and to these should be added our anti-Chinese and anti-Japanese enactments.

As already indicated, the discriminations against aliens and particular alien races were originally removed chiefly by means of treaties with different foreign nations, but for most purposes, such treaties had become so general, prior to the organization of our country, that most of the common law disabilities had been regarded as removed, even independently of specific treaties, because of the growth of commerce and friendly relations between states. This circumstance is clearly indicated by such an early leading case as Ormichund *vs.* Barker,[*] decided in 1775, where the right of a Gentoo residing in the East Indies to be sworn in an English lawsuit according to the ceremonies of his own religion, was sustained, despite early authorities to the contrary, because required by the modernized common law, which considers the requirements of an expanding foreign commerce. Despite Lord Coke's statement that "all infidels are in law perpetual enemies, for between them, as with the devils, whose subjects they are, and the Christians, there is perpetual hostility and can be no peace," Justice Willes remarked: "But this notion, though advanced by so great a man, is, I think, contrary not only to the Scripture, but to common sense and common humanity. I think that even the devils themselves, whose subjects he says the heathens are, cannot have worse principles; and besides the irreligion of it, it is a most impolitic notion, and would at once destroy all that trade and commerce, from which this nation reaps such great benefits."

[*]Willes Repts., 538. Compare the very able recent opinion of the New York Court of Appeals written by Judge Cullen in Brink *vs.* Stratton, 176 N. Y. 150, holding it to be a violation of the Constitution to ask a witness if he is an agnostic.

There was, howeve., an occasional disability on the part of
aliens which survived, such as incapacity to own land, and this was
removed as to most foreign nations by treaties which our government entered into from time to time. These treaties, as will be
further seen hereafter, have also nullified numerous state laws and
even constitutional provisions, which have been enacted from time
to time, to curtail the rights and privileges of various races which
happened to become unpopular for one reason or another, notably
the Chinese. Many of the decisions of the Supreme Court of the
United States and other tribunals to this effect may be found collated in such works as Professor Moore's "Digest of International
Law,"[7] Butler's "The Treaty Power" and the numerous articles and
treaties called forth by our recent Japanese separate school agitation, notably papers contained in the "Proceedings of the American
Society of International Law at its First Annual Meeting, April 19
and 20, 1907." So common have treaties safeguarding rights of
alien subjects become, that we have been compelled to insert in
many treaties provisions according to subjects of particular countries all the rights of the most favored nation, with resulting complications with respect to particular "reciprocity" treaties or the
like, which the courts have been compelled to hold granted special
privileges for special considerations, and were not intended to be
embraced by grants of all the "rights of the most favored nation."

But this particular form of "race legislation" scarcely falls
within the scope of the present paper. Of course, our Supreme
Court has held that our treaties cannot reasonably be construed as
preventing the enactment of general statutes for the exclusion of
alien paupers likely to become public charges or alien convicts or
diseased persons.[8] We have also, on occasion, made special provision in our treaties for the naturalization of aliens who are not
covered by our general naturalization laws, for the latter were,
curiously enough, limited to *white* persons originally, and the only
other classes added thereto are persons of "African nativity or
descent," so that the yellow races, including Chinese, Japanese,
Burmese, Indians and others (but not the copper-colored native
Mexicans), are generally regarded as incapacitated from naturalization,[9] though this discrimination was doubtless intended originally

[7] Vol. IV, Sections 534-578.
[8] The Japanese Immigrant Case, 189 U. S. 86.
[9] Rev. St. U. S., Sec. 2169.

only against Negroes and Indians in tribal organization.[10] This item further indicates how indefinite and uncertain the meaning of some of this race discriminatory legislation is, in view of ever-changing opinions as to anthropology and ethnic classification. Note, for instance, Professor Wigmore's scholarly article in the "American Law Review" (1894), "American Naturalization and the Japanese," denying that the Japanese are Mongolians, which would itself have disposed of the controversy on the California law for separate schools for Mongolians.

Reference has already been made to the fact that the leading exceptions to our general policy against race discriminations in legislation have been furnished by the negro, the Chinese and the Japanese races. As regards the negro, we built up a mass of discriminations running counter to our English common law of the most far-reaching and serious character which it required the sacrifice of blood and treasure of the Civil War to overcome. Many of these discriminations may be conveniently studied in Hurd's "Law of Freedom and Bondage." The fourteenth amendment to the federal constitution had the effect of making the most serious of these null and void, not merely in favor of the negro, but in favor of other races and classes also.

Following in the wake of this amendment, civil rights bills were enacted by our federal congress and in several of the leading states of our country, affirmatively forbidding, under heavy penalties, discriminations on account of race or color, even in the use of inns, conveyances, theatres, etc., clearly indicating our national attitude towards such discriminations, even on the part of quasi-public agencies. But some of these federal provisions were declared unconstitutional as an encroachment upon state power,[11] though as state enactments they have been quite generally sustained in jurisdictions which enacted them.[12] Numerous state enactments, discriminating against certain races, particularly the three designated

---

[10]Compare paper by the writer on "Naturalization and the Color Line" in the "Journal of Am. Asiatic Association," February, 1007.

[11]The Civil Rights Cases, 109 U. S. 3.

[12]See People *vs.* King, 110 N. Y. 418 ; Baylies *vs.* Curry, 128 Ill. 287 ; Commonw. *vs.* Sylvester, 13 Allen (Mass.), 247 ; Ferguson *vs.* Gies, 82 Mich. 358 ; Cyclopedia of Law and Procedure, Vol. 7, p. 158, *et seq.*, "Civil Rights ;" Vol. 8, p. 1073-4, Constitutional Law, "Equal Protection of Law ;" General *vs.* Special Acts, Vol. 14, Lawyers' Reports Annotated, 583 ; 2 L. R. A. 577 ; 7 : 194 ; 11 : 492 ; 14 : 566 ; 6 : 621 ; 21 : 789.

ones, have been held to be unconstitutional in state or federal courts because of the federal constitutional and treaty provisions referred to, or because violative of state constitutional provisions against special legislation and denials of equal protection of the law.

The fact remains, however, that a large number of statutory distinctions on race lines, particularly as applied to the negro, have been sustained, chiefly in southern states, on the theory that illegal "discriminations" are not involved, if equal but separate and distinct facilities for different races are afforded, with respect to street and railroad cars, steamships, restaurants, theatres, schools and the like. In justification of such enactments, applicable particularly to the Negro, reference has been made to alleged differences in education, character, standing and habits of the two races, and fear of endangering white man's control of our institutions and government, if any different course were pursued. The post-bellum cases are being analyzed and collated in an extremely interesting series of articles on "Race Distinctions in American Law," by G. T. Stephenson, in the "American Law Review," beginning with the January-February, 1909, issue, and one of them has also appeared recently in the "American Political Science Review" for May, 1909, entitled "The Separation of the Races in Public Conveyances." It is difficult, however, to escape the conclusion that they are inconsistent with the spirit of American government.

Our federal Chinese exclusion laws date from 1882 on, though we have had federal enactments against enforced, involuntary introduction of "coolies" from China, Japan or other Oriental countries from 1862 on.[13] The decisions of the Supreme Court of the United States have repeatedly and emphatically recognized what was conceded in our diplomatic negotiations and in our legislative debates, that "it is the coming of Chinese laborers that the act is aimed against"[14] merely, and the danger of competition from cheap coolie labor is the sole attempted justification for such laws requiring serious consideration.

Even in legislating for the exclusion of Chinese laborers, treaty faith and moral obligations required exemption of those who had *bona fide* come over in reliance upon the express provisions of the Burlingame Treaty of 1868 with China, whether laborers or non-

[13] See Rev. Statutes U. S., Sections 2158 to 2164.
[14] U. S. vs. Mrs. Gue Lim, 176 U. S. 459, 467.

laborers. By that treaty we had welcomed such immigration in express terms not paralleled in any convention with any other country, having even employed the opportunity to preach a text to China and the world concerning, to use the language of Article V, "the inherent and inalienable right of man to change his home and allegiance, and also the mutual advantages of the free migration and emigration of their citizens and subjects, respectively, from one country to the other, for purposes of curiosity, of trade, or as permanent residents." We also guaranteed, in Article VI, to "Chinese subjects visiting or residing in the United States, the same privileges, immunities and exemptions in respect to travel or residence, as may there be enjoyed by the citizens or subjects of the most favored nation."

Exemption under the constitution also had to be made of persons of Chinese extraction born here. Alleged difficulties in the enforcement of these laws and attempted evasions thereof—scarcely sustained, however, by our official government census, which recorded 105,465 Chinese residents in 1880, 106,000 in 1890 and only 93,000 in 1900, with 70,000 the present official estimate of the Department of Commerce and Labor—led to legislation for the registration of all resident Chinese laborers, under heavy and previously unheard-of extra-constitutional penalties, and danger of arrest of all Chinese, on the claim that they should have registered, and stringent, often unobtainable, proof on the part of all non-laborers was demanded. The law was administered on the theory that only "teachers, students, merchants or travelers from curiosity" may enter. The exclusion of "bankers," "traders," physicians, actors, etc., because not affirmatively enumerated, was ordered. The determination by administrative officers of all applications to enter was made final, with no right of resort to the courts on the difficult and important questions of law and fact involved, even with respect to claims to American citizenship. Uncontradicted evidence was disregarded in a way not sustained in any other class of cases; arrest and detention and a shifting of the burden of proof upon defendants, wholly abhorrent to our Anglo-Saxon system of jurisprudence, was practiced and held to be constitutional, despite bills of rights, on the theory that the right to exclude and expel aliens may be pursued by extra-constitutional methods. In short, there was instituted a constant reign of terror for all Chinese or alleged Chinese residents, laborers or non-laborers. Their liberty is constantly jeopardized by harsh and oppressive laws, and their property is accordingly also endangered under the sentiment thereby engendered that they are beyond the protection of our laws. Only one who, like the writer, has become familiar in practice with the injustice and barbarity of these laws in their actual practical workings, can realize that such practices can exist amid our boasted American civilization. The Chinese have little access to our public prints and have substantially no votes, and when even their officials, vehemently but righteously decline to join in doing honor to a military officer who had made an unauthorized extension of these anti-Chinese enactments to our new Asiatic possession, to breed such race prejudice on that continent, too, they become *persona non grata!*

Mr. Bryce, in his "American Commonwealth," published an interesting chapter entitled "Kearneyism in California," in which he showed how the unfortunate Chinaman became a victim of political exigencies which enabled his economic rivals, or rather persons who were led by interested leaders to believe that they were his rivals, to "deliver" control of the State of California to those who would most effectively discriminate against him. Already in 1855 and 1858 California passed laws to exclude Chinese immigrants, which its courts declared unconstitutional,[15] and in 1878 the United States Supreme Court was compelled to declare unconstitutional a California statute, passed some years before, covertly aiming to exclude Chinese persons by state agencies,[16] and both parties in the national election of that year demanded Chinese exclusion. Federal treaties and constitutional provisions annulled many hostile discriminatory state statutes and municipal ordinances, and it became obvious that federal legislation alone could accomplish this purpose.

President Hayes declined to yield to this clamor, in the absence of Chinese consent to a modification of the subsisting treaty, which would have been thereby violated, and vetoed a bill to restrict Chinese immigration for this reason on March 1, 1879.[17] In his able veto message he said, even as to the time anterior to the Burlingame

[15] People *vs.* Downer, 7 Calif. 169.
[16] Chy Lung *vs.* Freeman, 92 U. S. 275.
[17] Veto Messages of the Presidents, p. 414.

Treaty: "Up to this time our uncovenanted hospitality to immigration, our fearless liberality of citizenship, our equal and comprehensive justice to all inhabitants, whether they abjured their foreign nationality or not, our civil freedom and our religious toleration had made all comers welcome," but, in the light of the new conditions, he pointed out that a remedy could properly be found only in the negotiation of a new treaty, to permit the restriction of Chinese immigration consonant with international faith. China was thereupon induced to enter into the treaty of 1880, by which she consented to measures by which the United States was permitted "to regulate, limit or suspend such coming (of Chinese laborers), but . . . not absolutely prohibit it," "the limitation or suspension shall be reasonable, and shall apply only to Chinese who may go to the United States as laborers, other classes not being included in the limitation."

Under authority of this treaty we passed our first Chinese exclusion act, dated May 6, 1882, after President Hayes, on April 4th of that year, had vetoed another bill which violated the treaty, but the agitation did not cease. In 1884, under cover of "protecting" non-laborers, we violated the treaty by prescribing a statutory certificate for non-laborers, which is difficult to obtain, will not suffice if the officials made it out incorrectly in any way, or did not also authenticate a translation, and may be demanded as exclusive method of proof at any time, under penalties of arrest and deportation. Soon the theory of exclusive enumeration of non-laborers in this treaty of 1880 was developed, to bar "traders," "bankers," "manufacturers," etc., on the theory that they are not non-laborers.

The violations of treaty effected by the act were carried still further by the act of October 1, 1888, which invalidated our official return certificates, armed with which Chinese laborers or alleged non-laborers had gone to visit China on business or pleasure, and also prevented Chinese wives or children from joining or rejoining husbands or fathers.

This was followed by the well-known "Geary Law," with its requirements for registration under heavy penalties, and extra-constitutional methods of expulsion in addition to exclusion. It authorized arrest without warrant or oath, by methods unconstitutional in all other cases, and shifted the burden of proof to the defendant, in violation of our whole Anglo-Saxon methods of jurisprudence.

Then there came the act of November 3, 1893, giving an arbitrary and unjust definition of "merchant," and requiring white testimony, commonly impossible to secure, and proof of non-laboring by a "universal negative," which logicians teach us it is always impossible to establish. The act of 1894 made the decisions of the immigration officials—commonly ignorant, biased petty officials, acting as both advocates and judges—on the complicated questions of law and fact involved in applications for entry, whether right or wrong, non-reviewable in the courts, with the result that thousands of Chinese persons were unjustly dealt with, before the courts could decide some of these questions, in collateral proceedings, in their favor. Next the act of 1902 legalized the then subsisting situation as to the enforcement of these harsh laws in our insular possessions also.

The treaty with China of 1894, by which China is supposed to have consented to the Geary law provisions in a clause in unconscious irony describing them as passed for the benefit of Chinese laborers "with a view of affording them better protection," in return for authorization of return of Chinese laborers resident here, visiting China for brief periods under onerous condition, was terminated by China pursuant to its terms in 1904, making the violations of treaty faith guaranteed by the subsisting treaties of 1868 and 1880 worked by subsisting statutes, now still more glaring. As to the much-discussed exclusive enumeration theory of classes of non-laborers, who alone are permitted to enter, it is interesting to turn to the treaty negotiations themselves and to the testimony of Chester Holcombe, secretary and interpreter to this very treaty commission, to learn that no such result was intended, and the decision of Judge Ross to the contrary[18] in California in U. S. *vs.* Ah Fawn, 57 Fed. Rep. 591, approved by the Circuit Court of Appeals of that Circuit in Lee Ah Yin *vs* U. S., 116 Fed. Rep. 614, is of extremely doubtful correct-

[18]Holcombe: "The Question of Chinese Exclusion," "Outlook," July 8, 1905, and "Coolies and Privileged Classes," by the present writer, in "Journal of Am. Asiatic Association," March, 1906; on the general question of Chinese Exclusion, see also the present writer's paper in the "New York Times," Nov. 24 and 25, 1901, reprinted in Senate Document No. 106, 57th Congress, 1st Session; also his papers "Our Chinese Exclusion Policy and Trade Relations with China," "Journal Am. Asiatic Association," June, 1905, and July, 1905. See also Moore's "International Law Digest," Vol. IV, Sections 567-568; Butler's "The Treaty Power" and U. S. Senate Report and Testimony on Chinese Exclusion, No. 776, 57th Congress, 1st Session, 1902, as well as Letter from Minister Wu Ting Fang, printed as Senate Document No. 112, 57th Congress, 1st Session.

ness; the U. S. Supreme Court has never passed upon the question, and in fact seems to have thrown doubt on the correctness of the contention. (U. S. *vs.* Mrs. Gue Lim, 176 U. S. 459, 463.)

Both President Roosevelt and Secretary Straus have officially condemned the principle as unwise. Of course, however, both executive and law officers of the government find themselves compelled to follow these unreversed judicial decisions, especially in a matter having such important political bearings, even when against their own judgment. This circumstance accounts for much oppression in the enforcement of these laws.

It should, moreover, be remembered that even the Supreme Court is bound to enforce a statute, though it be clearly inconsistent with a prior treaty, despite our responsibility in the forum of international law and the resulting moral obliquity, and the court has several times contented itself with placing the responsibility where it belongs. One of the most serious consequences of such legislation is, moreover, the spirit it engenders of breach of national faith at the behest of supposed temporary expediency. Moreover, in making these laws peculiarly racial, by expressly making them applicable even to persons of Chinese extraction who are subjects of other nations,[19] we have violated treaties with other countries as well, and run the risk of further international entanglements.

A reference in passing to recent statutes authorizing the expulsion, within three years after landing, of any aliens for alleged specified causes by mere administrative action, with right denied of judicial review, indicates how invidious is the atmosphere which engenders such legislation. It creates a dangerous condition for all aliens and alleged aliens, in placing their rights on an administrative footing inferior to those of citizens, contrary to the American spirit.[20] On the other hand, as regards Chinese residents, it should not be forgotten that the statutory discriminations against them and their testimony and their subjection to irresponsible petty executive officers, has created a spirit of disregard for their persons and property of a very far-reaching character, and has resulted in their often becoming the victims of official bribery and extortion, to which Oriental races may be peculiarly susceptible. This cannot be measured

[19] Sec. 15 of the act of July 5, 1884.
[20] The Japanese Immigration Case, 189 U. S. 86, Justices Brewer and Peckham dissenting.

merely by the already appreciable number of convictions and dismissals of government officials for these causes, that happen to have taken place. It is but fair to say, in this connection, that there have been but comparatively few wholesale arrests of resident Chinese under our exclusion laws since the famous Boston raid of Sunday, October 11, 1902, when about 250 Chinese persons, in fact all the Chinese residents of Boston who could be found, were simultaneously arrested, nearly all to be subsequently discharged, after sustaining gross hardships and injuries. Hon. John W. Foster has ably described this contemporary imitation of the "Black Hole of Calcutta," and the large public meeting of protest in Fanueil Hall following it, in an article on "The Chinese Boycott," in the "Atlantic Monthly," January, 1906.

It was thought by the present writer than an account of the conditions created by these legislative race discriminations by one like himself,' familiar with them for fifteen years might be more effective than any generalizations and abstract arguments.

Fortunately, the dangers from attempting to include the Japanese in these same special measures at the behest of a recently aroused anti-Japanese sentiment on the Pacific Coast have, for the time at least, been averted, by securing friendly action on the part of the Japanese government at home in the direction of preventing Japanese laborers from immigrating to the United States. This is accompanied by an enactment of general applicability, adopted February 20, 1907, for the exclusion of persons covered by Presidential proclamation, who are required by their own laws to secure passports to come to the United States. The reports of the Commissioner General of Immigration for the years ending June 30, 1907 (pp. 72-76), and June 30, 1908 (pp. 125-128), and of Secretary Straus for 1908 show how effective these regulations have been, not simply in excluding applying aliens of the class in question, but in preventing them from even applying or attempting to enter. In connection with proposed Japanese exclusion, Professor Royce's recent suggestive and ironical words are extremely apt:[31] "The true lesson which Japan teaches us to-day is that it is somewhat hard to find out, by looking at the features of a man's face or at the color of his skin or even at the reports of travelers who visit his land, what it is of which his race is really capable. Perhaps the Japanese are not of the

[31] Race Questions and Prejudices and Other American Problems. 1908, p. 14.

right race; but we now admit that so long as we judged them merely by their race and by mere appearance, we were judging them ignorantly and falsely. This, I say, has been to me a most interesting lesson in the fallibility of some of our race judgments." So, also, in his extremely interesting and suggestive paper, "The Causes of Race Superiority," included in the ANNALS OF THE AMERICAN ACADEMY OF POLITICAL AND SOCIAL SCIENCE, Vol. 18, 1901, Professor Edward A. Ross well said, before emphasizing the real elements of race superiority: "We Americans who have so often seen the children of underfed, stunted, scrub immigrants match the native American in brain and brawn, in wit and grit, ought to realize how much the superior effectiveness of the latter is due to social conditions."

To return, however, to the Chinese exclusion problem: It is apparent that the desire to exclude the Chinese laborer has worked incalculable harm both to them and to us, at least in excluding non-laborers and causing much unnecessary and unintended hardship. If cheap pauper labor, competing on unequal and unfair terms with American labor be involved, such labor can be excluded under general laws, not applicable to the Chinese merely, and not making exclusion the rule and a few enumerated classes of non-laborers the exception. It must be apparent, however, to justify even such reversal of our established beneficent and satisfactory American policy of a century and more, that the danger be general and continuous, and not temporary and spasmodic, and that it is one that cannot be cured by effective distribution, so as to deprive sections needing such labor badly, of the benefits to which they also are entitled. It should take reasonable form, and not be oppressive, unequal and confusing. Nor should it be dictated by spite and caprice, unworthy of a great state or nation, and designed merely to vex and annoy or to discriminate.[22]

Fortunately, President Roosevelt, his Secretary of Commerce and Labor, Mr. Straus, and President Taft, while Secretary of War, have all expressed themselves emphatically on this subject in the

---

[22]Note California's famous anti-queue law (Ho Ah Kow *vs.* Nunon, 5 Sawyer, 552); her anti-Chinese disinterment law (*In re* Wong Yung Qay, 2 Fed. Rep. 624); her special Chinese tax law (Lee Ging *vs.* Washburn, 20 California, 534), and constitutional prohibition of employment of Chinese by corporations (*In re* Tiburcio Parrot, 1 Fed. Rep. 481), and compulsory removal requirement to new sections (*In re* Lee Sing, 43 F. R. 359), and anti-Chinese-fishing law (*In re* Ah Chong, 2 Fed. Rep. 733).

direction of amelioration of our subsisting Chinese exclusion acts, and the substitution of general laws on the subject, and their utterances accord on this point with those of his Excellency Wu Ting Fang. In the course of an interesting address delivered by the last-named at Ann Arbor University more than eight years ago, the Chinese Minister well said: "The exclusion of Chinese is brought about, you are probably aware, by special and not by general laws. It is a discrimination against the people of a particular country. . . . If, however, it be considered advisable to legislate against the coming of laborers to this country, let such a law be made applicable to all Asiatics and Europeans as well as Chinese. . . . The Chinese immigration question is a complicated one. To solve it satisfactorily is not easy. It is necessary to look deeply into the subject, and not allow oneself to be swayed by prejudice and bias. Prejudice is the mother of mischief, and injustice, and all intelligent men should guard against it."[23] In any event, however, it is only the Chinese laborer that the laws are even intended to exclude, and the laws should obviously be recast so as to exclude merely this particular class and not the whole race, with only a few specified exceptions, making admission the rule, not the exception.

The Chinese boycott of 1905 against American goods called attention forcibly to China's deep resentment of our exclusion policy and of the serious injury it had wrought to our commerce and the imminent danger of reprisals. Our mercantile interests were therefore enabled to compel new and independent consideration of this policy on the part of President Roosevelt and his advisers. On June 24, 1905, President Roosevelt directed a vigorous letter to the State Department, requiring more humane treatment for the Chinese and caused the Department of Commerce and Labor to issue a circular to its subordinates to the same effect   The following October, in an address at Atlanta, he outlined his own policy in the matter, but pointed out that he cannot do all that should be done without action by Congress, action which has not yet been taken. In his message to Congress of December 5, 1905, he said: "In the effort

²³This address contains a very valuable discussion of the services rendered by the Chinese to America, and combats the economic arguments against Chinese exclusion. I quote it from a pamphlet entitled "Truth versus Fiction, Justice versus Prejudice," also reprinted in Senate Document No. 106, 57th Congress, 1st Session. See also his letter, Senate Document No. 162, 57th Congress, 1st Session, and also the able article by Ho Yow, late Chinese Consul-General at San Francisco, in the "North American Review," September, 1901.

to carry out the policy of excluding Chinese laborers, Chinese coolies, grave injustice and wrong have been done by this nation to the people of China and therefore ultimately to this nation itself. Chinese students, business and professional men of all kinds—not only merchants, but bankers, doctors, manufacturers, professors, travelers and the like—should be encouraged to come here and be treated cn precisely the same footing that we treat students, business men, travelers and the like of other nations. Our laws and treaties should be framed, not so as to put these people in the excepted classes, but to state that we will admit all Chinese, except Chinese of the coolie class, Chinese skilled or unskilled laborers. . . . There would not be the least danger that any such provision would result in the relaxation of the law about laborers. These will, under all conditions, be kept out absolutely. But it will be more easy to see that both justice and courtesy are shown, as they ought to be shown, to other Chinese, if the law or treaty is framed as above suggested."

Secretary Taft was the first official spokesman of the Roosevelt administration to express similar views, on the occasion of an address at Miami University, Oxford, Ohio, on June 15, 1905. He stated that we cannot escape the charge of having broken Chinese treaty rights by our legislation. In the effort to catch in the meshes of the law every coolie laborer attempting illegally to enter the country, we necessarily expose to danger of contumely, insult, arrest and discomfort the merchants and students of China who have a right to come to this country under our treaties. We must continue to keep out the coolies, the laborers; but we should give the freest possible entry to merchants, travelers and students, and treat them with all courtesy and consideration. Two years after the boycott, Mr. Straus, in his first report as Secretary of Commerce and Labor for 1907, said even more specifically: "It has never been the purpose of the government, as would appear from its laws and treaties, to exclude persons of the Chinese race merely because they are Chinese, regardless of the class to which they belong. . . . The real purpose of the government's policy is to exclude a particular and well-defined class, leaving other classes of Chinese, except as they, together with all other foreigners, may be included within the prohibitions of the general immigration laws, as free to come and go as the citizens or subjects of any other nation. As the laws are framed, however, it would appear that the purpose was rigidly to exclude persons of the Chinese race in general, and to admit only such persons of the race as fall within certain expressly stated exemptions—as if, in other words, exclusion was the rule, and admission the exception. I regard this feature of the present law as unnecessary and fraught with irritating consequences. . . . Laws so framed can only be regarded as involving a discrimination on account of race, and it is needless to point out that discriminations on account of race, color, previous condition or religion are alike opposed to the principles of the republic and to the spirit of its institutions."

In his annual report as Secretary for 1908 he said: "The invidious distinctions, to use an apt phrase, now so apparent on comparing the treatment of necessity meted out to Chinese with the treatment accorded to aliens of other nationalities, in my judgment would not exist but for the fact that the subject of Chinese immigration is distinguished from all other immigration by being dealt with in a separate code of laws, involving a wholly distinct mode of procedure—a mode, moreover, which is at once cumbersome, exasperating, expensive and relatively inefficient. . . . Essentially the entire question involved in the admission or exclusion of Chinese is not a distinct and independent matter of legislative regulation, but in reality is merely a part of the larger problem of immigration."

I cannot conclude better than to quote a stimulating passage recently written by Professor Royce, that distinguished psychologist and student of races, as to the dangers of race discrimination, in a paper on "Race Quesions and Prejudices:" "Let an individual man alone, and he will feel antipathies for certain other human beings very much as any young child does—namely, quite capriciously—just as he will also feel all sorts of capricious likings for people. But train a man first to give names to his antipathies, and then to regard the antipathies thus named as sacred merely because they have a name, and then you get the phenomena of racial hatred, of religious hatred, of class hatred and so on indefinitely. Such trained hatreds are peculiarly pathetic and peculiarly deceitful, because they combine in such a subtle way the elemental vehemence of the hatred that a child may feel for a stranger, or a cat for a dog, with the appearance of dignity and solemnity and even of duty which a name gives. Such antipathies will always play their part in human history. But what we can do about them is to try not to be fooled by them, not to take them too seriously because of their mere name. We can remember that they are childish phenomena in our lives, phenomena on a level with the dread of snakes or mice, phenomena that we share with the cats and with the dogs, not noble phenomena, but caprices of our complex nature."

REASONS FOR ENCOURAGING JAPANESE
IMMIGRATION

By JOHN P. IRISH,

Naval Officer of Customs for the Port of San Francisco, Cal.

Whether the United States should any longer encourage any immigration is doubtful. That the United States should treat all immigration alike is far less doubtful, since it implies a policy that makes for international peace and our own national dignity. Agitators, themselves of alien birth, originated opposition to Asiatics in California prior to 1860. In the legislative session of 1861 a committee that had been previously appointed to that duty, reported upon an exhaustive investigation of the effect here of the presence of Chinese. After a statistical statement and an array of economic facts, the committee said:

"We are confident that these facts will deeply impress you and our constituents, and it will be well to ponder them before any action shall be proposed that will have a tendency to disturb so important an interest, and drive from our state a class of foreigners so peaceful, industrious, and useful. Your committee trust that no more legislation will be had calculated to degrade the Chinese in our state."

That report settled the question for many years, until it became the subject of agitation on the "sand lot" late in the seventies. When that report was made the population of California was 379,994, of which 50,000 were Chinese, the only Asiatics then here. Carrying out the proportions of our present population we should have 300,000 Asiatics, but we have only 55,904 Chinese and Japanese combined.

Since the agitators have directed their efforts against the Japanese almost exclusively, it is noted that favor for the Chinese has risen. All of the arguments formerly made against them are now directed against the Japanese. It is of historical interest that these arguments are all taken bodily from the campaign of persecution of the Jews in continental Europe from the Middle Ages down to modern times, when civilization and enlightenment effected the emancipation of that mistreated race.

As for immigration in general, we have acquired the habit of saying that none should be admitted with which we cannot assimilate. This has put upon our Anglo-Saxon blood the mighty task of assimilating the alien peoples of Southern and Southeastern Europe, and we are recently learning that assimilation is a bilateral process, and that the vast influx of those peoples who are in semi-racial accord with us, is diluting our original stock and that instead of assimilating we are being assimilated. Economic pressure has expelled European immigrants from their native soil, and they have resorted here in such numbers as to overcome our prepotency and even threaten changes in our institutions.

In view of this it is well to consider whether the charge that the Japanese are non-assimilable, and therefore should be excluded, has any merit. The Japanese are, like us, a temperate zone race, with a form of civilization high in its essentials and much older than our own. It is doubtful whether the term "coolie" in its usual sense applies to them. The common people of Japan, as we know them here, more nearly resemble the Irish peasantry than the East Indian coolie. They are very industrious, frugal, temperate and orderly, with quick wit and intellectual alertness. By the standards established by our immigration laws and the regulations for their enforcement, the Japanese are desirable immigrants, judged by the amount of money they bring with them, the percentage that seek aid in public hospitals and eleemosynary institutions, and their percentage of illiteracy. Upon these points the official immigration records give the following testimony:

MONEY PER CAPITA.

Japanese	$31.09	Polish	$11.51
South Italians	10.96	Scandinavian	26.52
Irish	26.42	Slovak	13.75
Hebrew	15.36	Magyar	14.03

PER CENT RECEIVING PUBLIC AID

Japanese	.007	Greek	.81
South Italian	.73	German	.99
Irish	.52	Polish	1.04
Hebrew	1.62	Scandinavian	.3

PERCENTAGE OF ILLITERATES

Japanese	22.	Polish	36.
South Italian	54.	Hebrew	23.
Greek	24.	Russian	26.
Portuguese	68.	Lithuanian	54.

Labor and Wages

The Southern European immigration inveterately congests in our cities. The Japanese take kindly to rural life and productive farm labor. In California the Latin races are numerous in the coast cities. They skip the great valley, which is the seat of varied agricultural and horticultural production, and reappear in the Sierra foothills and mountains, around the mining towns and lumber camps.

In the delta of the Sacramento and San Joaquin rivers, and in the Great Valley of California, is the demand for rural labor which the Chinese formerly supplied, and, as their number decreases under exclusion, the demand is now met by the Japanese. The production of raisins, sugar beets, asparagus, onions, and other low growing field crops, and the fruit harvest, call for reliable labor, resistant to climatic conditions and able to sustain the stooping posture in which much of this work must be performed. So far American labor has not proved efficient or reliable in these occupations, and European labor is but little more so. But the short-backed, short-legged Asiatics have proved reliable in all this squat work which must be performed in a temperature of 100 to 110 degrees. They execute the needful primary processes in these forms of production, and thereby furnish commerce with merchandise which in its transmutation, transportation and exchange provides for American labor occupation at its own high wages, and for commerce its profit. This fact is recognized by the fruit growers of California, who, in their annual convention in 1907, by unanimous vote, demanded such modification of the Chinese exclusion law and of the anti-Japanese policy as would permit a certain immigration of both races.

A critical examination of the subject in respect to its industrial, economic and social phases, supports the legislative report of 1861, that the presence of Eastern Asiatics here is of industrial, economic and social benefit to the state. Japanese farm laborers have notable characteristics, of which their personal cleanliness is especially to be noted. They require facilities for a hot bath, and at the close of a day's labor they bathe and change to dry clothing before eating dinner.

Japanese farm labor by the month exacts $1.50 per day wages. The largest farmer and largest employer of farm labor in California is Mr. George Shima, a Japanese, who pays an annual rental of $80,000 for lands farmed on the leveed islands in the delta of the Sacramento and San Joaquin rivers. In his vast operations he employs American, Japanese, Chinese and European labor, getting the best results by such co-ordination of labor. His American and European laborers are paid the going wage and are employed in the work that precedes and follows the primary processes of tillage performed by Japanese. His Japanese labor is paid by the year. His common laborers get $250 per annum and "found" in their work clothing, diet and dormitory. His Japanese foremen are paid $350 and found. In good years he pays to laborers and foremen a bonus in the nature of profit sharing. While he has brought about this co-ordination of labor, the system has now been adopted by American employers. The sugar beet fields are plowed, prepared and planted by American labor at high wages, using the best improved agricultural machinery. When the beets grow they must be thinned by hand and weeded for a space on each side of the row. This, being squat labor, is performed by Japanese and by Chinese when they can be had. The American labor reappears in cultivating the crop, riding, spring seated, on improved implements. At the harvest the Japanese reappear, and from that time on the crop furnishes highly paid work to American labor until it reaches the consumer.

Investors in the beet sugar business here insist that as the squat part of the work is performed when the temperature is high, it is so repugnant to American labor that Japanese are a necessity, and that by this co-ordination of labor only is it possible to develop this valuable resource of the state.

The Japanese standard of living in their own country of course cannot escape the economic law, but is fixed by the wages of labor. To this law all countries are subject. Up to the beginning of the Irish exodus to the United States, laborers' wages in Ireland were six cents per day, sometimes rising to eight cents. But the standard of living, long fixed by low wages, rose when the Irish came in contact with better conditions here. The same is true of the Japanese. They live well. The laborers when at leisure dress well, in our costume. When one by two or three years' work has accumulated from $500 to $750, he is enterprising, and usually sees some overlooked resource in which he invests his savings and labor and advances rapidly. In all these respects he differs not at all from the immigrants from other low wage countries, except in his superior enterprise and greater adaptability. As farmers the Japanese excel. The lessons learned at home are applied here, and the land is made to produce crops, not weeds. No slipshod methods are followed, and Americans may beneficially apply the lesson they may learn of Japanese farmers.

Education

A very considerable percentage of Japanese laborers are students, eager to learn. When they acquire English and read it, their leisure is employed in reading our works on history, biography and science. This tendency is not observed in other immigrants. They laboriously work their way through our public school grades and universities by farm labor or domestic service. Of their qualities as students the following opinion is given by one of the oldest public school principals in San Francisco:

(1) I have had ample opportunities, in over twenty years' experience with Japanese students, to know whereof I speak, in all its bearings.

(2) No considerable part of these students are adults. Had the adult pupils ever reached as large a proportion as twenty per cent there would, years ago, have been protests from teachers and principals, and Japanese adults could and would have been excluded from elementary day schools, just as are other adults, without friction or objection.

(3) Japanese students do not crowd white children out of the schools. The San Francisco schools are not overcrowded. They never have been overcrowded, during the past twenty years, except in a few spots, and that for causes entirely outside this matter.

(4) The statement that the influence of the Japanese, in our schools, has had a tendency towards immorality, is false, and absolutely without foundation. From all I have ever heard in conference with other school men, as well as from my own continuous and careful observation, there has never been the slightest cause for a shadow of suspicion affecting the conduct of one of these Japanese pupils. On the contrary, I have found that they have furnished examples of industry, patience, unobtrusiveness, obedience, and honesty in their work, which have greatly helped many efficient teachers to create the proper moral atmosphere in their class rooms.

(5) Japanese and American children have been on good terms in my class rooms, and in others concerning which I am informed. They work

side by side without interference or friction, and often some Japanese student would be a great favorite among his American classmates.

(6) In all my years of experience, there has never come to me, orally or in writing, from the parents, whose children have attended my school, one hint of complaint or dissatisfaction concerning the instruction of their children in the same school, or the same rooms with Japanese. Nor has there ever been complaint or protest from teachers in regard to this co-education.

International Ethics

To include Japanese in the Chinese exclusion laws will raise grave international issues. Japan has adopted western civilization, and her civil institutions are tempered by the parliamentary system. Her jurisprudence is based on the common law and conforms to the English standard which is the foundation of ours. In science she has impressed the world by the results of original investigation. The world now has the means of escape from bubonic plague, because the Japanese bacteriologist, Kittesato, discovered the plague germ, revealed its biological progress and the means of its transmission from rodent to man. Another Japanese bacteriologist isolated the dysentery microbe and caused a reduction of fifty per cent in the mortality from that scourge of armies. The world cannot set the seal of inferiority upon a nation that has furnished such men. Nor can it afford to judge Japanese by the classes that are lowest in the scale.

Japanese friendship for America is of undoubted sincerity. When San Francisco was destroyed by earthquake and fire, and her people were in extremity, lacking food and shelter, Japan sent for their relief $245,000, the only foreign nation that came to their rescue, though France has recently sent a medal.

Japanese business men and financiers resident here are in every way acceptable. Their home life is characterized by refinement and good taste. Their wives are ladies, many of them college graduates, who understand and observe the social conventions. The presence of this commercial and financial class is necessary to our trade with Japan. It is the destiny of that country to become to Asia what England is to the western world and to draw upon exports from the United States to an equal degree. Every consideration seems to counsel a policy of peace, good will and equality of treatment toward Japan. In the case of the Japanese, there is no room for race prejudice, but every inducement to a policy of justice and amity.

MORAL AND SOCIAL INTERESTS INVOLVED IN RESTRICTING ORIENTAL IMMIGRATION

By Rev. Thomas L. Eliot, S.T.D.,

President, Board of Trustees of Reed Institute, Portland, Oregon.

The middle Pacific northwest, so far, has not been invaded by Chinese and Japanese in large numbers, and, except for a brief agitation in 1886, our Portland community has had little share in the passionate oppositions which the advent of these peoples has caused farther south, and to a degree in the British north. This fact might at the outset seem to disqualify us in the present discussion. A Californian can say, with a certain truth, "Your conditions farther north are not as yet attractive to the Oriental. There are with you no exploitations of labor, no such exigencies of harvest times to draw laborers together in masses, and no organizations directly promoting immigration as there are with us. We have decidedly more manufactures and capitalization of irrigated lands. The cry for cheap labor is exigent, and we are therefore confronted with conditions of immigration from the east which appal us. This invasion is supplanting the white population, actually eating us out; and it is accompanied by all manner of moral and social degradations."

But, on the other hand, it appears to many of us that our southern friends by their very nearness to the problem are formidably biased in their judgment. In fact, the imagination of some of their leading writers has run riot. The proximate industrial disturbance and the irregularities of the newcomers are conjured into nightmares of the future Orientalization, not only of the western coast, but of America itself. Perhaps the most marked example of this "stage fright" may be seen in an article which appeared in "Collier's Weekly" some months since and has been widely copied and commented on throughout the entire country. The essay is entitled "Orientophobia," and is from the pen of one of the ablest and sincerest editors of the Californian press, writing from the midst of an area where the Japanese are colonizing most rapidly. It must be granted that the tone of Mr. Rowell's paper is forceful and rushing—no one who is discussing the question can afford to pass him by. At the first perusal the facts recounted, the fears summoned up, the pessimistic drive and the prophetic warnings of the writer fairly sweep one along, and seem to compel assent. As an example of torrential eloquence, it is almost unequaled. Every subsequent perusal, however, led me to qualify its note and to distrust the author's generalization and conclusions. It dawns upon one that he is proving too much. There may indeed be a world crisis, the greatest since Thermopylae and Salamis, confronting the Pacific coast of America, and no doubt the whole case of the United States with the Negroes of the south, and the ceaseless stream of immigration from Europe, together with the threatenings of Oriental clouds presents a mighty problem; but why may it not be regarded as a challenge to all the higher forces of civilization for some safe and triumphant solution, rather than as a portent and depression? Is it a time for building Chinese walls, and shutting ourselves in as Japan once did, or is it an age of social engineering, for the invention of powers of control, adjustment, and distribution? What is there in the problem to daunt the trained intelligence, the wisest statesmanship and the social enthusiasm of the nation?

For, the one undeniable fact which seems to be emerging is that a certain growing number of Orientals is to be on our shores, partly floating, and partly to stay. It is almost equally certain that exclusion is frankly impossible, deportation impracticable, and the lines of restriction are more, and more difficult to define. Others will discuss what may and ought to be done in order to regulate the quantity and quality of the immigration. No doubt careful legislation is necessary both east and west, and in the west, at least, labor immigration should be made the subject of more and more careful treaties and comities with China and Japan. But in the outcome, there will be an accumulation of these peoples, determined to be here by economic principles, and attaching themselves to the soil according to the industrial demands of city and country life. To the present writer it seems a fairly open question whether the ratio of Orientals to the rest of the white population will increase. Except for limited areas, there are with us on this coast no such conditions historically and economically as in the Hawaiian Islands—that is a problem to itself. A few checks and balances added to the present restriction laws ought to suffice for the maintenance of the present ratio on the basis of the entire coast. At the same time the quality of the immigration might be advanced.

The real problem lies with the hosts rather than the guests; as a problem of resourcefulness, adaptation and character. Shall these immigrants be antagonized, solidified into a caste, driven in upon themselves, compelled by our very treatment of them to herd vilely, and live viciously, or shall there grow up among us in the interest of moral and social sanity a determination to minimize crass-race-prejudice, to dissipate the superstitions and ignorances of both whites and non-whites, and to set up assimilating processes as far as possible along the levels of individual merit and higher efficiencies? Shall we foster the very evil we dread, or shall we somehow foster the germs of good will? Shall our legislation be panicky and steady-by-jerks, or shall it be enlightened and progressive; shall the laws be administered evasively, or evenly, in the interest of peace and progress or of race and class conflict? Do not authors of articles like this "Orientophobia," all unwittingly perhaps, accent the notes of antagonism and invoke passion, mob violence and war with foreign powers, through their insistence upon a theory that race difference and repugnance are irreducible, and through their failure to note the real limits of the problem, or to count up the real resources of a true civilization? When they trumpet for a "white man's frontier," to be maintained if necessary by war and lines of garrisoned fortresses, they are but repeating what helped to foment the riots of the thirties against the Irish, and the opposition of the middle west to the "damned Dutch." In spite of their rude reception, these races, as well as the Scandinavian and other northern races, have been measurably assimilated without any sensible deterioration of the mass; the "hordes" of Southeastern Europe are, if we may trust reliable reports, in a similar process of assimilation, to be delayed, or to be hastened, in the measure that forces of sympathy and education prevail or are withheld.

Even admitting that Orientals are in a different class, what real reason is there for prophesying that they and white races cannot live upon the same soil, use the same language, and in time share each other's mental and social ideals? The process of co-operation will not be difficult when once the alternative course is fairly faced and its consequences fully realized in imagination. For the alternatives are sanguinary and brutalizing. It takes but little imagination to depict the future if the Chinese and Japanese are given over to mobs, and are refused justice; if they are traduced, denied education and civic rights, if they are treated as animals, and are barred all humanities and amenities. For such abuses, both soon and late, there will be a fearful reckoning. A complete estrangement from us of eastern nations, with all that is involved of commercial loss, and the possibility of war, are the least of the evils thus invoked. The greater evil would be visited upon our national character, for in shutting our doors and persecuting inoffensive immigrants, we would have surrendered to mob power, and the mob yielded to always means increasing inhumanity and injustice poured back full measure into the bosoms of those who were their instructors. All the more would such retributions heap up for us, when the chief charge we can bring upon the Oriental, is that, class for class, he is cleaner, thriftier, more industrious, and docile, better bred, better trained, and better mannered than his white neighbor in the world of labor and life.

These views will be called academic, and whoever holds them ought frankly to admit his own limitations. The exclusionist and high restrictionist have the apparent advantage of figures and experience, and can always plead "the present distress." They seem on solid ground when they appeal to the instincts of race purity and of self-preservation. They alone, perhaps, realize the hardships and strains put upon communities and individuals, when the competition of labor seems to drive the better men to the wall. But it must be repeated, those who are mixed up with a problem do not always see the best way out. They cannot understand the need of sacrificing a nearer benefit, to the larger principle. Theirs is the shortsighted view perhaps in this very case, which once drove the Moors out of Spain to the lasting injury of peninsular civilization, which blinded all Southern France in the silk weavers' riots to fight the newly-invented loom; and which united the squireocracy and agricultural laborers of England against the first steam railroads. Economic history is full of such hardships of progress and sufferings of adjustment. The peril is always a great one, that sympathy with those who suffer, may blind rulers and peoples to greater coming good for greater numbers, including it may be even the present sufferers. In the very nature of society, if progressive, there is always a fighting line where the unskilled labor of society is to be done, and another fighting line where the highest leadership is to be achieved, where the greatest principles of civilization are trying to win out. Over this conflict and friction, the will of the whole people as expressed in good government, in wise legislation, in impartial enforcement of the laws, in enlightened study of conditions should insure civilization against retrogressive steps.

The problem of immigration, especially in the shape in which it is presented to Western America, should be placed in charge of an expert governmental commission of the highest class, with ample powers, capable of patience and detachment from prejudice, in order to formulate all the facts and propose the practicable solution of how the civilization of the west and the east may meet, and how they may mingle—since mingle on some terms they must—with advancing good will and the mutual attainment of material, moral and social good.

This is the challenge that the situation presents to united America. The east as well as the west is concerned in answering it upon the highest lines of national and international harmony. When we ask ourselves what grounds of encouragement there are to hope that an honorable solution will be reached, it needs but to rehearse some of the achievements, over equally stubborn problems lying all about us, and to measure up the new pace which is set for education, for enlightenment, for solidarity of national sentiment, for new evaluations of human lives, and above all for the obligations of society towards its weaker members.

Civic consciousness is growing everywhere. The conviction that material wealth must be harnessed to great uses of state, that culture and knowledge of every kind constitute responsibility and must serve the public, the consciousness that every neglected class or individual endangers the mass and may poison any other individual or class, these are the dynamic truths pushing the imagination, stirring the wills of men. The social conscience which is leading the fortunate to give away so many millions yearly to endow colleges, libraries, hospitals, foundations of research; which creates the Nobel prizes, the Cecil Rhodes bequests, the Russell Sage trust and others is supplemented by state and municipal action in order to give cities nobility, comfort, beauty and wider opportunity. Who would have been bold enough to prophesy, even twenty years ago, that Boston would expend $20,000,000 in a park system, and Chicago would provide recreation halls and playgrounds for the common people costing $10,000,000? Let some of the same conscience and trained intelligence be turned to conditions of immigration, promoting the welfare of the newcomer and providing adequate channels of distribution, let as much be done to make the immigrant more American, as is now doggedly done to keep him un-American, above all let as much be done to defend him from the pirates of sea and land who prey upon his ignorance and helplessness, as is now unhappily left undone—then should we not have a right to hope, at least, that our great problem would turn out a side to the light, and become illumined with human cheer?

WHY OREGON HAS NOT HAD AN ORIENTAL PROBLEM

By F. G. Young,

Professor of Economics and Sociology, University of Oregon, Eugene, Ore.

Early Oregon did not offer to the Oriental opportunities for exploitation that bore any comparison to those afforded by California. On the discovery of gold San Francisco became the great entrepôt to which all vessels from the Orient turned, and stray delegations from the swarming ports of China were soon borne to the new Eldorado. San Francisco's channels of trade and lines of employment yielded largest streams of gold,—the sole lure of emigrants from the Celestial Empire.

The dearth of women and children among the rapidly growing aggregation of adventurers that constituted the main body of San Francisco's population not only left open to the Chinaman just the vocations for which he shows special aptitudes, but created as well the strongest demand for his services. He came as the complement necessary to make immediately a community out of a horde of the gold-seekers of the fifties. In the older Oregon community to the north the conditions were those of a staid agricultural settlement, quite in contrast to those developed by the mining activities of California. Oregon was made up of transplanted households of home-seekers. It afforded neither an opening nor a considerable demand for the Oriental's services. There was no lure of high wages nor large earnings in any line of employment, nothing to compare with the attractions which the California metropolis held out.

The main lodestone that was soon to draw the large influx of Orientals to California was the gold-bearing gravel beds back of San Francisco along the streams of the Sierras. John Chinaman quickly learned that the income secured through washing these was even larger than the returns from washing dishes or clothes down in the city. So to the recesses of the mountains he flocked and soon accumulated a hoard with which he returned to his native land and became the cause of the coming in turn of many others. Oregon's first instalment of Chinese was received as soon as the placer diggings within her southern borders were disclosed. To these they came in numbers to constitute a considerable proportion of the early population of her sparsely settled southern counties. But they came direct from California and thither returned without obtruding themselves on the main body of Oregon's population in the Willamette Valley to the north.

Naturally at first Oregon's ratio of Orientals, compared with that of her neighbor's to the south, was small. In the later fifties and sixties, while there was still great activity in placer mining in California, the proportion of Chinese among her population was at least ten times as great as that of Oregon. From the later seventies on, however, the California percentage has not been twice that of Oregon and the census figures for 1900 make the comparative number in California barely larger than that of Oregon. It is to be noted that with a quota of Mongolians constantly growing, so as relatively to be almost equal to that of California, the public mind in Oregon has remained calm while in California there has been continual trepidation.

A more impressive illustration of the comparative equanimity of Oregon in view of her situation is, however, afforded through a comparison of Oregon's quota of Orientals with that of Washington on the north. Oregon has always had a larger contingent of Chinese and Japanese in her population than Washington—and generally it has been two or three times as large. Outbreaks in acts of violence have occurred there, while the people of Oregon have regularly maintained conditions of peace and order.

At no time has public feeling in Oregon run so strong against the Oriental as in the communities to the north and south. Except once or twice, when stirred by sympathy with what was happening among her neighbors, Oregon can hardly be said even to have had a consciousness of the problem. There has been only sporadic agitation instigated by emissaries from without, and no riotous outbreak.

It thus becomes an interesting question to account for a response, so in contrast, to a situation she has largely in common with her neighbors. Oregon's serenity is probably partly due to certain social characteristics of her people and partly to the peculiar circumstances attending the presence of the Orientals within her borders. Oregon has never had any considerable element of ignition tinder in her population in the form of a large body of floating wage-earners. With such present, and a large element of Orientals, occasion for a conflict is sure to arise. The presence of such elements in San Francisco after the completion of the Central Pacific Railroad and the oncoming of the depression of the early seventies, and likewise in Tacoma and Seattle after the finishing of the Northern Pacific in the period of stagnation in 1885, was necessarily fraught with trouble. A congregated mass of idle white men feeling the pangs of want would resent the slightest competition on the part of an alien race. It would be treated as an intruder. Permanent prejudice would be engendered. When Tacoma effected the expulsion of the Chinese and a faction in Seattle undertook the forcible deportation of them in February, 1886, Portland naturally was stirred. The balance of influence was, however, so clearly on the side of law and order that the mischief-making forces desisted. Because of the slower and more steady development of Oregon no large number of homeless wage-earners have ever been caught adrift here. It is to the absence from her population of a large admixture of such inflammable elements that the lack of any heat of resentment against the Chinamen within her borders is to be attributed. No experience of trouble, no inter-racial clashes from such sources brought to her thought the consciousness of an Oriental problem.

A contributing factor making for immunity from the consciousness of such a problem—and one also of a negative character—is, or rather was, to be found in the sluggish commonwealth spirit in Oregon. The menace to the standard of living of the laboring classes involved in the presence of a considerable body of Orientals has of course been patent to the thoughtful. These have discerned, too, the burden and blight in the presence of an alien social element. But until recently very little facility has been possessed by any class for securing concert of movement for the public welfare. Neither the agency of the state government nor voluntary organization could be brought into requisition for the discussion, investigation and improvement of a social condition. The Oregon people, or any contingent of them, were slow to get together in co-operation for the public welfare. So there was no anticipation of a problem from conditions not wholly normal.

Turning now to the peculiar circumstances that have attended the presence of the Oriental in Oregon: The objective conditions have all been of a nature to leave the resentment of the white man unaroused. As already mentioned, the first influx sought the placer mines of Southern Oregon. The jealousy of the white miner was shown in a heavy special license tax upon Chinamen engaged in mining and absolutely prohibitive fines upon any trading by them. A constitutional provision adopted in 1857 debarred them from the ownership of mining property. The irritation caused by their presence must, however, have been mollified by the substantial revenues collected from them for a decade in four or five southern counties.

Oregon, in common with the other Pacific coast and inter-mountain communities, has not been able to draw to any extent upon European immigrants for domestic and other menial services. The manning of the salmon canneries, the furnishing of garden truck for the cities, and the supplying of the "section hands" for the railroads, have also been occupations for which the white wage-earners of this part of the country had no relish. Such vocations were freely accorded to the Mongolians. The Oregon quota of Orientals year in and out has just about sufficed to meet the demand in these undesired employments. The Chinaman has been aptly termed "the nigger of the coast." However, he is far above the Negro in habits of industry, cleanliness and other virtues, and brings no troubles upon himself through pernicious political aspirations. Representative captains of industry here have even urged that there should be a change from the exclusion of the Chinese laborer to a policy of a limited immigration for a term of years in order to supply a desirable labor force for expediting the clearing of areas for farm crops.

Under the present operation of the exclusion policy towards the Chinese no apprehension whatever is felt about them. It is the Japanese whose incoming is not so securely barred and whose power of organization is effective that are regarded as a very probable menace to the future peace and highest destiny of the Pacific coast. They are rising in the industrial scale and are securing leases and even ownership of real estate. Few will deny that if they are given an equal chance with the white man here their stronger social cohesion and more effective co-operation would win for them a perma-'nent foothold. The rapid extension of the fruit growing industry in Oregon would also furnish an opportunity for which the Japanese in California have proven that they have strong adaptation. So with regard to the Japanese, while it can hardly be said that there is the consciousness of a problem yet in Oregon, it must on the other hand be confessed that to throw open the doors to the inhabitants of Nippon and to order commonwealth affairs wholly on a commercial basis, would probably develop in a few years a situation fraught with a problem of no slight proportions.

PART THREE

National and International Aspects of the Exclusion Movement

TREATY POWERS: PROTECTION OF TREATY RIGHTS BY FEDERAL GOVERNMENT
BY WILLIAM DRAPER LEWIS, Ph.D.,
DEAN OF THE LAW SCHOOL, UNIVERSITY OF PENNSYLVANIA, PHILADELPHIA

THE PROBLEM OF ORIENTAL IMMIGRATION IN THE STATE OF WASHINGTON
BY HERBERT H. GOWEN, F.R.G.S.,
LECTURER ON ORIENTAL LITERATURE, UNIVERSITY OF WASHINGTON, SEATTLE, WASH.

THE EFFECT OF AMERICAN RESIDENCE ON JAPANESE
BY BARON KENTARO KANEKO,
TOKIO, JAPAN

CHINESE LABOR COMPETITION ON THE PACIFIC COAST
BY MARY ROBERTS COOLIDGE,
FORMERLY ASSOCIATE PROFESSOR OF SOCIOLOGY, STANFORD UNIVERSITY, CAL.;
AUTHOR OF "CHINESE IMMIGRATION" (IN PRESS)

THE LEGISLATIVE HISTORY OF EXCLUSION LEGISLATION
BY CHESTER LLOYD JONES, Ph.D.,
INSTRUCTOR IN POLITICAL SCIENCE, UNIVERSITY OF PENNSYLVANIA, PHILADELPHIA

HOW CAN WE ENFORCE OUR EXCLUSION LAWS?
BY MARCUS BRAUN,
IMMIGRANT INSPECTOR, DEPARTMENT OF COMMERCE AND LABOR, WASHINGTON, D. C.

ENFORCEMENT OF THE CHINESE EXCLUSION LAW
BY JAMES BRONSON REYNOLDS,
NEW YORK CITY

TREATY POWERS: PROTECTION OF TREATY RIGHTS BY FEDERAL GOVERNMENT

By WILLIAM DRAPER LEWIS, PH.D.,

Dean of the Law School, University of Pennsylvania, Philadelphia.

Mr. Bryce in his "American Commonwealth" points out that the Federal Constitution as it now stands, "with the mass of fringing decisions which explain it, is a far more complete and finished instrument than it was when it came fire new from the hands of the convention."[1] The truth of this assertion is evident to the student of our constitutional law. At the same time it must be remembered that, while the Supreme Court has "fringed" much of the text of the constitution with explanatory decisions, there yet remain many parts, and these by no means always of comparative unimportance, which have never been interpreted by the court, or on which there is still much room for speculation, in spite of the fact that they have been interpreted to some extent by our supreme judicial tribunal. Again, the fact that the framers did not attempt to describe the manner in which the powers conferred on the different departments of the federal government should be exercised, and "the laudable brevity" of the constitution have been made, and justly, the subject of favorable comment. But here, too, we must admit, that though the skill with which the constitution was drawn makes it one of the really great achievements of our race, it is not equally perfect in all its parts. Brevity and the statement of general principles not only may but do, in parts of the constitution, degenerate into intolerable uncertainty as to the real principle intended to be enunciated. In dealing with more than one subject of vital importance the language and the arrangement leaves room for wide speculation. As a result of this inequality in the skill of construction and in the amount of judicial interpretation, though we can ascertain with great particularity the answer to almost any question pertaining to certain clauses of the constitution, as, for example, the clause which gives Congress the power to regulate interstate and foreign commerce or the clause prohibiting the states from passing a law impairing the obligation of contracts, we are unable to give even a reasonable guess as to what would be the answer of the Supreme Court to many questions —and some of these of first importance—pertaining to other parts of the constitution. Unfortunately, there is perhaps no part of our fundamental law which is open to such diverse interpretation and which has received so little illumination from the court as that which relates to the treaty-power.

The second clause of the second section of the second article of the constitution provides that the President, "shall have power, by and with the advice and consent of the Senate, to make treaties, provided two-thirds of the Senators present concur." The second section of the sixth article provides: "This constitution and the laws of the United States which shall be made in pursuance thereof, and all treaties made, or which shall be made, under the authority of the United States, shall be the supreme law of the land; and the judges in every state shall be bound thereby, anything in the constitutions or laws of any state to the contrary notwithstanding." What is the nature of this treaty-power conferred on the President and Senate? When a treaty is negotiated and ratified does it become of its own force "the supreme law of the land" or is an act of Congress approving it or expressing its provisions necessary to give it the force of law?

It has been assumed by most of those who have studied the constitution that the very words of that document show that it was supposed by the framers that treaties would be self-executing. Thus, the second section of the sixth article treats the constitution, the laws of the United States, and treaties, as three distinct and separate sources of "supreme law." The second section of the third article, in conferring judicial power on the United States, also assumes the existence of these three distinct sources of "law," declaring that "the judicial power shall extend to all cases, in law and equity, arising under this constitution, the laws of the United States, and treaties made, or which shall be made, under their authority." Any doubt, however, which might exist on this subject has apparently been put at rest by the Supreme Court, which has, in a number of cases, regarded treaties as the "supreme law."

though no act of Congress had been passed sanctioning their provisions.[2]

When we turn from the nature of the treaty-power to its extent we find greater possibilities for divergence of view. At the
same time even here there is a general agreement on certain propositions. In the first place, it is apparently beyond question that the
grant of treaty-power in the second article of the constitution is
much more sweeping than the grant of legislative power in the
first article. Congress is declared, not to have the power to make
laws, but merely the power to make laws on certain enumerated
subjects. On the other hand, the President and Senate have the
power "to make treaties," the subject of a treaty, as far as the
second article is concerned, being left entirely to their discretion.
At the same time there is also a substantial agreement on the
equally self-evident proposition that the constitution, like a contract
between a principal and his agents, must be read as a whole, and
that there may be, and are, limitations on the treaty-power to be
found in other clauses of the constitution. For instance, the amendments from the second to the eighth inclusive enunciate certain
individual rights and declare in general terms that these rights
shall not be infringed. The rights so protected can no more be
disregarded in a treaty than in an act of Congress. Again, the
constitution provides to a certain extent for the organization of
the federal government. The first article deals with the selection,
organization and power of Congress; the second, in a somewhat
similar way, with the executive; and the third, with the judiciary.
It is admitted by all that the treaty-power can no more be exercised to alter this organization established by the constitution than
the organization so established can be altered by an act of Congress. Neither can a power granted by the constitution, as the
power to regulate interstate commerce, be in anywise modified by
treaty. This, of course, is not saying that the treaty-power cannot
also deal with those things over which Congress is granted legislative power. The question whether the powers granted to Congress over certain subjects exclude the exercise of any control of

²Chirac *v.* Chirac, 2 Wheaton's Reports, 259 (1817); Orr *v.* Hodgson, 4
Wheaton's Reports, 453 (1819); Hughes *v.* Edwards, 9 Wheaton's Reports, 489
(1824); Carneal *v.* Banks, 10 Wheaton's Reports, 181 (1825); Hauenstein *v.*
Lynham, 100 United States Reports, 483 (1879).

these subjects by treaty is another and a different matter on which there is much difference of opinion. But all admit that a treaty regulating commerce which provided that Congress should have no power to alter its provisions by subsequent legislation would be, to the extent of this proviso, null and void.

There are many provisions in the constitution, however, the effect of which, if any, in limiting the treaty power is open to dispute. As an example of this class, we may take the second to the seventh clauses of the ninth section of the first article. The sixth clause, for instance, provides: "No money shall be drawn from the treasury, but in consequence of appropriations made by law." Suppose a treaty provides that a sum of money shall be paid; could the President take the money from the treasury without the sanction of an act of Congress? The writer would give a negative answer to this question, and such answer would be in accordance with the uniform practice of our government. At the same time, it can with some reasonableness be urged that these prohibitions are part of the first article of the constitution; that this article in its preceding sections has dealt only with the organization and power of Congress; that the first clause of the ninth section in terms prohibits, not all departments of the federal government, but "Congress" from interfering with "the migration or importation of such persons, as any of the states, now existing, shall think proper to admit, prior to the year one thousand eight hundred and eight"; and that, therefore, the prohibitions in the remaining clauses of the ninth section should be construed as limitations on Congress only. On the other hand, the prohibitions contained in these clauses are not in terms confined to prohibitions on legislative action, and that the evidence taken from the rest of the first article is not sufficiently conclusive to show an intent that they should be so limited. The tenth section prohibiting, as it does, the states from entering into "any treaty, alliance, or confederation," and from passing "any bill of attainder, *ex post facto* law, or law impairing the obligation of contracts," shows that "law," whether by treaty or by act of Congress, is dealt with in the first article, and indicates that any restrictions in the article which are not in terms restrictions on Congress or the states should be regarded as general restrictions on all departments of the federal government.

A more difficult and doubtful question, however, is whether

any or all the powers granted to Congress in the eighth section of the first article are or are not exclusive? This question in any of its possible phases has never come before the Supreme Court. The practice of the government, when the question has arisen, has been to act as if the powers of Congress over matters entrusted to it by the first article were exclusive, and that a treaty dealing with any of these subjects, as, for instance, a treaty regulating custom duties, must have the sanction of an act of Congress before it can be regarded as the "law of the land." Even then if the power over imposts is, as contended, exclusive in Congress it is improper to call the treaty the "supreme law;" the "supreme law" is rather the act expressing or approving the terms of the treaty.[5]

To the writer the constitution of the United States should be interpreted from the point of view of an instrument creating for the people different agents on matters of vital importance. General treaty power is given to certain agents, the President and the Senate; particular legislative power is given to Congress. Whether any particular grant of power to Congress over a subject is to be taken as prohibiting an exercise of any control over that subject by the President and Senate in the form of a treaty, should depend, when there is no express direction in the constitution, on the nature of the subject. If it is a subject ordinarily only dealt with by legislative bodies, then it is reasonable to assume that the particular grant of control to Congress withdraws that subject from the treaty power. Now the great majority of the subjects over which Congress is given control fall under the category of subjects practically never dealt with by treaty. For instance, the power to lay and collect taxes, to coin money, to establish post offices and post roads, to constitute inferior judicial tribunals, to make rules for the government of the land and naval forces, all 'of these subjects and many more, control over which is granted to Congress, have rarely if ever been made the subject of contract between nations. Control over them having been given to Congress, we may infer that it was intended that the control should be exclusive. On the other hand, foreign commerce is a common subject of treaty and the

[5]For a history of the practice of the government see "Limitations on the Treaty-Making Power of the President and Senate of the United States," by Prof. Wm. E. Mikell, reprint from University of Pennsylvania Law Review, pages 13 et seq.

mere fact that Congress is given the power over foreign commerce should not be interpreted as curtailing the President and Senate from exercising a similar control in a treaty.

Whether the reasoning above indicated is or is not sound, whether the treaty power has or has not the right to deal with all or some or none of the subjects over which Congress has legislative power, though questions of importance, are not questions of fundamental or vital importance. Treaties require for their ratification a two-thirds vote in the Senate. It is unlikely that a treaty desired by two-thirds of the Senate would be disapproved by a majority of the House. It is probably easier to secure the passage of an act of Congress which requires only a majority in both houses than to secure the ratification of a treaty. We may be also fairly certain that a sufficient number of senators will always be found to adopt the theory that all powers granted to Congress are exclusive, to prevent the ratification of a treaty which deals with any subject entrusted to Congress by the first article of the constitution without the passage of an act authorizing the treaty. The questions are not of fundamental importance because their decision one way or the other does not deprive the United States of the power to make agreements with foreign countries touching all matters delegated to Congress. If such agreements cannot be made by treaty, they can be embodied in an act of legislation.

A far more vital difference of opinion arises over the question whether there are any limitations on the treaty power arising from what are known as the reserved powers of the states. The preservation of these "reserved powers" was the object of the tenth amendment. The amendment provides: "The powers not delegated to the United States by the constitution, nor prohibited by it to the states, are reserved to the states respectively, or to the people." Those reading this amendment in connection with the first and second articles of the constitution seem to follow one of two trains of reasoning. The intellectual descendant of Jefferson argues: The government of the United States is one of delegated powers. True, it has the power to make treaties; but on what subjects? It was not the intent of those who adopted the constitution to confer on the federal government power over their local affairs and police. The tenth amendment prohibits such an inference. Those who assert that the federal government has that power must show some express grant. What are the powers delegated to the United States? They are those powers conferred on Congress by the first article, and, by necessary implication, the power to deal with matters external to the states. The schools of Hamilton and Marshall base their conclusions on a literal interpretation of the words of the constitution. That the United States is a government of limited power is admitted, but it is pointed out that the powers granted are to be determined, not by a supposed intent, but by the words used. The President with the concurrence of two-thirds of the Senate has power to make treaties. The tenth amendment treats of powers not delegated to the United States. The treaty power is delegated and, therefore, by the very words of the amendment outside its scope.[4]

The decisions of the Supreme Court in as far as they have involved the question should be noted. In Chirac v. Chirac,[5] the court held, that the treaty of 1800 between the United States and France giving to French citizens the right to inherit land in the United States, superseded the law of Maryland which denied this right. Here is a decision that the federal government by treaty can deal with a subject not proper for federal legislation, and which relates to a matter which is not external to the states. More recently the Supreme Court in the case of Hauenstein v. Lynham[6] held, in spite of a law of Virginia to the contrary, that a citizen of Switzerland had, under our treaty with that country, the right to the proceeds of the sale of land in Virginia. These are the most important cases, though there are others of similar import.[7] In none did counsel or court contend that the federal government had not the right to negotiate the treaty or that when ratified it was not the supreme law of the land. Judge Swayne in Hauenstein v. Lynham, above cited, states the attitude which, without the felt necessity for explanation and defense, has always been taken. He says, "In the able argument before us, it was asserted upon one side, and not denied on the other, that if the treaty applies its efficacy must necessarily be complete. The only point of contention was one of construction."

[4] If the reader is anxious to examine the view first expressed he will find it set forth with pains and skill by the writer's associate, Prof. Mikell, in the article referred to, *supra*, note 3. The second view has recently been stated and defended by Senator Root. See 1 American Journal of International Law, 273.
[5] 2 Wheaton's Reports, 259 (1817).
[6] 100 United States Reports, 483 (1879).
[7] See cases cited, *supra*, note 3.

From these decisions we may conclude that it is settled law that the treaty power can be so exercised as to confer on aliens rights to property in the states which could not be conferred by act of Congress. They also settle in the negative the sweeping contention that the tenth amendment prohibits the treaty power from dealing with all matters not delegated to Congress and relating to the internal economy of the states. A treaty can be negotiated and ratified which will supersede state laws relating to rights of private property. On the other hand, it has never been held by the Supreme Court that the tenth amendment has no effect in limiting the treaty power. The question, for instance, whether the treaty power can be so exercised as to supersede state laws relating to health and morals has never been decided. It is true that there is apparently nothing in the text of the constitution to warrant a line being drawn between the power of the states to regulate the acquisition of real property, and the power to pass laws relating to gambling or diseased cattle, so that one could logically hold that the tenth amendment did not prevent the first class of laws from being superseded by treaty, but did prevent the last two classes of laws from being superseded. Law, however, is not necessarily logic; and besides, it must be remembered that a present member of the Supreme Court who believed that Chirac *v.* Chirac and Hauenstein *v.* Lynham proceeded on erroneous principles in disregarding the tenth amendment, while he might feel bound to follow these cases in a case presenting substantially identical facts, is not bound to follow what he regards as a wrong principle to all its logical consequences.

But even if we should regard the decisions which we have quoted as settling, forever, that the treaty power is in no wise limited by the tenth amendment, there is still another line of reasoning which renders uncertain the constitutionality of a treaty which would deal with matters subject to the police power of the states. using the term police power as including all laws which relate to the morals and the health of the people or their governmental organization and public activity. The constitution assumes the existence of the states. The states are as necessary a part of our federal state as the national government. All this is generally admitted, and from these admitted premises many students of the constitution draw the inference that any power granted to the federal government is subject to the implied limitation that it must not be so exercised as to destroy a state. It is probable that any treaty which affected the organization of a state government, which attempted to alienate without the consent of a state, part or all of its territory, or which gave to aliens the right to share in the property or services of a state, as the right to use the public parks or the right to attend the public schools, would be considered unconstitutional. Whether a treaty which gave rights denied by the laws of a state passed to protect the morals or health of its citizens would be constitutional to a person holding this theory of implied limitation of power is not so certain, though it is likely that a treaty which permitted an alien to reside in a state, contrary to the opinion of the state that he being white, or yellow, or black would contaminate the morals of the people, would be regarded as tending to destroy the state, and therefore by implication beyond the power of the United States to make the supreme law of the land. When once a person adopts the theory of grants or limitations of power which arise, not from the text of the constitution, but from "the nature of things assumed to exist by the constitution" he is embarked on an uncertain sea whose boundaries will depend on his instinct, or, at the best, on shifting theories of the essential nature of our federal state. The judiciary with their power to disregard acts or treaties contrary to the constitution become more than the interpreters of a written instrument; they become the self-appointed guardians of a spirit of the constitution which the framers omitted to embody in the letter.[8]

The Supreme Court as such has never said that these implied limitations on treaty power exist, but several individual members of the court have, in the past, denied the power to override the police laws of the states, though it is not clear whether the judges referred to took this position because of the tenth amendment or because of some theory of implied limitation of power.[9] The question is one of profound importance. If the treaties which run counter to state police regulations are not the supreme law of the land, any act of Congress which runs counter to a state police regu-

[8] For a discussion of this particular question see an article by the present writer in 55 American Law Register, entitled "Can the United States by Treaty Confer on Japanese Residents in California the Right to Attend the Public Schools?"

[9] See license cases, 5 Howard's Reports, 504, opinion of Daniel, J., p. 613; of Woodbury, J., p. 627; of Grier, J., p. 631; of McLean, J., p. 588. For other opinions along similar lines, see passenger cases. 7 Howard's Reports, 283.

lation is also of no effect. There is nothing, for example, peculiar in the power of Congress over interstate commerce, which would enable a law within the scope of this power, to override a law passed within the scope of the states police power, if a treaty within the apparent scope of the treaty power could not have that effect.

This summary of the uncertainties surrounding the extent of the limitations on the treaty power of the federal government shows the state of unfortunate confusion which exists as to its limitations. It is possible for one to hold any one of three theories:

First.—That as a result of the tenth amendment matters subject to the legislative power of the states, and not subject to any legislative power conferred on Congress are not subject to the treaty power.

Second.—That the treaty power is impliedly limited by the dual nature of our federal state; that the power cannot be so exercised as to interfere with the police powers of the states, using the term "police power" as including control over the organization of government, public property, public services, morals and health.

Third.—That the treaty power is not limited either by the tenth amendment or by any implied reservations arising from the nature of our federal state.

A fourth position is possible; namely, that the treaty power is limited by the tenth amendment as indicated in the first proposition, and also impliedly limited as indicated in the second proposition. The great practical difference in the results flowing from the adoption of one rather than another of these theories, will be seen if we apply each in turn to treaties purporting to confer rights on aliens.

Under the first theory we can by treaty confer on aliens the right of travel in any part of the United States, but not any rights of a resident in a state. The power of Congress to regulate interstate and foreign commerce has been given an interpretation sufficiently wide to make an act, and, therefore, under the theory a treaty, a regulation of commerce which relates to the journeying of persons, whether foreigners or citizens between the states, or between the United States and foreign countries. But a treaty guaranteeing to an alien any rights of residence or any protection as a resident would be beyond the federal government to make effective, because a law purporting to protect a citizen of the United States, resident in a state, from assault is beyond the power of Congress to enact, and, therefore, under the theory beyond the treaty power. Likewise, a treaty purporting to confer on the citizens of a foreign country, being resident in that country, the right to make contracts with the citizens of the United States would be constitutional, because such contracts would also come within the power to regulate commerce with foreign nations; but once let the foreigner become a resident of a state, and if the laws of that state denied to foreigners being residents, the right to contract or to obtain property, or placed special restrictions on their commercial intercourse, no treaty could protect them. Their only redress, and it would be one of very doubtful efficacy, would be that portion of the first section of the fourteenth amendment of the constitution which provides; "nor shall any state deprive any person of life, liberty or property without due process of law, nor deny to any person within its jurisdiction the equal protection of the law."

If we adopt the theory that the treaty power is limited by the very nature of our federal state, and also that as a result, the power cannot be so exercised as to interfere with the exercise by the states of their police power in the sense in which we have defined that term, any treaty conferring on aliens rights of travel, or residence would be powerless to confer on an alien the right of travel or of residence in any particlar state except subject to those rules which the state regarded as necessary to preserve the morals, health and safety of its citizens. For instance, a state law which arbitrarily excluded all foreigners might be superseded by a treaty admitting the citizens of a particular country, but a state law which obliged all persons of African descent to reside in particular parts of a city, or to ride in "Jim Crow" cars would apply to a negro subject of Great Britain, traveling in that state, even though a treaty in terms stipulated that all persons being subjects of Great Britain should in traveling and residing in the United States, be subject only to those laws and regulations which pertained to white American citizens. In short, he who believes a treaty cannot supersede a state law passed under its police power might admit that a treaty would require a state to treat an alien, except as to political rights, as if he were a citizen, but he would probably claim that a treaty can confer on an alien no greater rights than those he would have if he were a citizen of the United States.

Lastly, if we adopt the theory that the tenth amendment in no wise limits the treaty power, and also deny any implied reservations on that power not found in the text of the constitution but arising from the nature of the federal state called into being by the adoption of the constitution, then all treaties granting to aliens rights of travel or residence in the states, or guaranteeing to them while residents protection from injury, and even treaties conferring rights in conflict with the police laws of the states, and vesting foreigners with the right to use the public property and obtain the public services of the states, would be constitutional. Of course, that treaties giving many of the above rights to aliens would be constitutional does not mean they might not violate that spirit of respect for local desires which should always influence the exercise by the national government of the powers entrusted to it. That a treaty which would override the reasonable laws of a state passed in good faith to protect the health or morals of her people, could be negotiated under present conditions by any President, or ratified by a two-thirds vote of any Senate is unthinkable. But the fact that a power may, theoretically, be abused is not an argument that it ought not, still less that it does not, exist. Generally, any power entrusted to government adequate to meet critical emergencies in legal theory may be used to defeat the very ends, the preservation of the nation, for which it was conferred.

When we turn from the nature and extent of the treaty power to the extent to which the federal government can protect rights granted by treaty we approach a subject on which, fortunately, there is little room for radical difference of opinion. The third section of the second article makes it the duty of the President to "take care that the laws are faithfully executed." He is also, by the second section of the same article, made "commander-in-chief of the army and navy of the United States." If a treaty is self-executing, it has when ratified by two-thirds of the Senate the force of law, and the President in the exercise of his constitutional duty "to take care that the laws be faithfully executed" has the right, unless prohibited by Congress, to use as a means to this end the army and navy of the United States. Congress by law may indicate the occasions when the army and navy shall be used, but in the absence of legislation the President has, under the constitution complete discretion to use the military forces of the United States to execute its laws, subject only to the limitation that he cannot violate any general prohibition expressed in the constitution, as the prohibitions expressed in many of the amendments.

The President in executing his duty of enforcing a treaty, as in enforcing any law, is not limited to the employment of the military. He can use any other means which Congress has seen fit to place at his disposal. Thus, if Congress has created a secret service, and not by express provisions confined its use to subjects other than the enforcement of rights guaranteed by treaty, the President has the right to use the service to discover plots which if carried out would violate those rights.

Again, the President can call to his assistance any person or persons willing to lend such assistance. For instance, if a mob in one of our cities were about to assemble at a station to prevent aliens from getting off the trains on which they arrived, contrary to a treaty giving to them the right of travel in the states, the President could call "on all law-abiding citizens" to protect, by force, if necessary, the right of the aliens to leave the train The citizen responding to the call would, of course, be liable if in attempting to enforce the treaty he violated a legal right. It is, to say the least, doubtful if Congress by legislation could prevent the President from securing voluntary assistance in the exercise of his constitutional duty to enforce law.

Finally, the President has the right to use any appropriate legal process for the enforcement of law, and therefore of treaties. The judicial power of the United States, by the second section of the third article "extends to all cases in law and equity arising under treaties made, or which shall be made, under their authority." But the extent to which any court of the United States may act depends wholly on affirmative congressional action. Congress not having made the violation of a right conferred by treaty a crime, the courts of the United States have no criminal jurisdiction over any alleged violation; and the President is at present without power to institute any criminal proceedings for the violation of a treaty right. Again, there is at present no law which gives the President a right to institute a suit for civil damages for the violation of such a right. General equity jurisdiction has, however, been conferred on the courts. By general equity jurisdiction we mean that jurisdiction which was exercised as a matter of custom by the High

Court of Chancery in England. In the main the nature of the jurisdiction is preventive. A person threatened with the violation of a
right for which no adequate remedy in a suit for damages exists
may bring a "bill in equity" praying that an injunctive order issue
to restrain the threatened violation. By custom also, the attorney-
general of England on behalf of the state could bring bills in equity
to redress certain public wrongs. When, therefore, it is said that
the courts of the United States have general equity jurisdiction we
imply that the attorney-general of the United States may at the
instigation of the President and on behalf of the United States
bring any bill which the attorney-general of England could bring
on behalf of the English government in the High Court of Chancery. The customary equity jurisdiction does not extend to all
public wrongs; that is to say because an act is a violation of law
does not necessarily 'enable the attorney-general to bring a bill in
equity for its restraint. But by custom the jurisdiction of a court
of equity does extend to the restraint of those wrongs which injure
public property or which amount to a public nuisance. The word
nuisance in this connection has received a wide interpretation. It
means any act which prevents a number of persons in a community
from exercising a right. If, therefore, a treaty guaranteed to all
the citizens of Great Britain rights of residence in the United States,
and we regard such a treaty as within the power of the President
and Senate, if one Englishman resident in a state was denied those
rights by anyone or more persons being private persons or officers
of the state, a court of equity, while it might restrain the violation
of the treaty at the private suit of the Englishman affected, would
not entertain a bill in equity brought on behalf of the United
States by the attorney-general. To give the attorney-general a
right to bring the bill, a special statute requiring the federal courts
to take jurisdiction would have to be passed. On the other hand,
if there existed a movement on the part of one or more persons in
a state to deprive all English subjects of the rights guaranteed to
them by treaty, then such movement would constitute a public
nuisance and the President could require his attorney-general to
bring a bill in equity to secure an injunctive order restraining the
wrong.

We have so far spoken of the power of the President to enforce a lawful treaty in the absence of any legislation by Congress

especially designed to insure obedience to treaties on the part of all persons within the United States. It is as certain as any proposition can be which has not been directly formulated by the Supreme Court in a case involving its application, that Congress has been given by the constitution power to pass any law legitimately designed to strengthen the enforcement of any treaty which it is within the power of the President and the Senate to make. The eighteenth clause of the eighth section of the first article not only gives to Congress the right "to make all laws which shall be necessary and proper for carrying into execution the foregoing powers" —meaning the legislative powers conferred in the preceding seventeen sections—but it also confers the right to make all laws which shall be necessary and proper for carrying into execution "all other powers vested by this constitution in the government of the United States, or in any department or officer thereof." The power to enforce the laws of the United States is a power vested in the President.

Acts designed to secure the enforcement of law may be roughly classed under three heads: administrative, penal and procedural. An act which would place at the disposal of the President, officers whose special duty it was to guard the persons of aliens would fall under the first class; a penal statute would be one which provided for the imprisonment or fining of anyone who violated any right given by treaty. Under the last head would fall any act which extended the jurisdiction of the courts of the United States in cases involving alleged violation of treaty rights, or any act which directed the procedure to be followed in any such case. For instance, an act which enabled the President to direct the attorney-general to bring a bill in equity for an injunctive order to protect an individual alien threatened with a violation of a right conferred on him by treaty would fall under this class.

Of course, these statutes must not violate any prohibition contained in the constitution. The administrative statute must not authorize those "unreasonable searches and seizures" prohibited by the fourth amendment; the penal statute must not deny to the accused "a speedy and public trial," contrary to the sixth amendment, and the procedural statute must not confer original jurisdiction on the Supreme Court contrary to the second clause of the second section of the third article. But within the limitations mentioned it is almost impossible to think of an act reasonably designed to enforce a treaty that would be unconstitutional.

That the act must be "reasonably designed to enforce the treaty" is clear. The constitution does not say that Congress shall have power to make any law which *it thinks* necessary and proper for carrying into execution a power vested by the constitution in any department or officer of the government, but merely that Congress shall have power to make those laws which shall be *necessary and proper* for carrying into execution a power vested. Under this grant Congress has a wide choice of means to be used; but the means must bear some reasonable relation to the end, which is the execution of the power, and the Supreme Court has the final right and duty to pass on the question whether the means used bears sufficient relation to the power to make it within the right of Congress to select that means to enforce the power. Take as a concrete instance: A treaty guarantees protection to aliens traveling in the United States. A federal statute making it a crime to attack an alien, as such, while traveling, contrary to the right conferred by the treaty, would be without question a proper means of enforcing the treaty. But suppose the act should go farther than this and make anyone who wilfully injured an alien subject to indictment. As in terms the statute supposed does not require that it must be shown that the accused knew that the person he injured was an alien, if A in a quarrel kills B, not knowing that B is an alien, he would, nevertheless, be indictable under the statute. The constitutionality of such a statute is far from certain. The end,—the enforcement of the treaty,—and the means,—the punishment of one who killed another whom he did know was an alien,—would, at least, in the opinion of the writer, fail to bear sufficient correspondence to sustain the act. The question, of course, is an academic one. It is not likely that Congress will ever in our day do more than make the wilful attack on aliens, as aliens, criminal.

Thus, the means which are unquestionably within the power of the federal government, if properly used, would appear to be ample to enforce all treaties. The doubts, and they are many which surround the subject we have discussed, are, as we have seen, as to the extent of the treaty power, not as to the right of the United States to maintain respect for, and punish violations of, those treaties which it may lawfully make.

THE PROBLEM OF ORIENTAL IMMIGRATION IN THE STATE OF WASHINGTON

By Herbert H. Gowen, F.R.G.S.,
Lecturer on Oriental Literature, University of Washington, Seattle, Wash.

One of the oldest legends of Japan tells of the sun goddess, Amaterasu, how she sulked and shut herself up in a cave till all the world was dark and fear possessed the hearts of men. Myriads of deities, the story goes on to say, did their best to induce the goddess to reappear, but without success. At last came the deity *Thought-Includer*, child of the *High-August-Producing-Wondrous-Deity*, who hatched a plot. Outside the door of the cave the conspiring gods made so mighty a noise, dancing and singing, that the goddess could not forbear opening the door ajar. Then they flashed in her face a wonderfully polished mirror, showing the goddess to herself, and while Amaterasu admired they closed the cave behind her. So the land again had light. The opening of Japan to intercourse with the outside world through the epoch-making visit of Commodore Perry has certainly in many respects brought Japan face to face with a new epoch in her history and has had results which those who lured forth the sulking goddess could scarcely have anticipated. A nation once out of the box is not easily to be recaptured and re-imprisoned.

The awakening of Japan is the awakening of the whole Orient. The huge bulk of China is responding as certainly, if more slowly, to the influences of western civilization as the more impressionable Island Empire. Already we perceive the feverish starts, the "impatient nerves which quiver while the body slumbers as in a grave."

This awakening at the present time finds few skeptical as to its significance. Professor Percival Lowell indeed, writing, however, before the Russo-Japanese war has endeavored to belittle its interest for ourselves by speaking of the Oriental civilizations as worn-out, decadent, exhausted. He has made himself believe that reaching the Pacific they have found Nirvana. But such an attitude can only remind us of the Japanese story given in a book of Buddhist sermons,—the story of the frog who journeyed from Tokio to see Kyoto and, reaching a mountain top midway, stood on tiptoe to view the western capital. He saw only the city he had left—*for his eyes were in the back of his head.* Recent events have more strongly than ever emphasized the fact that the Orient has by no means as yet satisfied itself with Nirvana. It is becoming more and more evident that, whether we are considering the general question of state policy towards an Oriental country or whether we are considering some local problem, such as that of immigration, which indirectly affects the general international situation, it is necessary to take this into account. The apparently isolated question of immigration is, like Thor's drinking horn, connected quite inevitably with the ocean of international considerations.

The attitudes of men with regard to the facts of Oriental development may quite reasonably vary. Some may, like the eloquent author of "The Torch," be bracing their souls to the contemplation of the distant future, when American civilization shall have played its part in the world's making and we, more or less resignedly, shall have to pour the accumulated treasures of history into the lap of the Eastern world.

Others may look at the whole matter, even from the American standpoint, optimistically, seeing in the meeting of east and west the completion of Hegel's great circle of spiritual development, the day's work of the "Ewigzeitgeist." Others again may view the future fearfully. As Anaxagoras unrolled before the Athenians the map of Anaximander, while he harangued them on the danger of the Persian advance, so these may lift up the cry of the "Yellow Peril" and color with alarmist pigments the counsels of statesmen and the editorial utterances of the press.

Whatever the attitude adopted, the country needs, even for the discussion of local problems, a broad appreciation of facts. On July 12, 1852, Mr. William H. Seward pointed out that two civilizations which had parted company four thousand years ago on the plains of Asia were meeting again on the Pacific. Hence, he added, "the Pacific Ocean, its shores, its islands and the vast regions beyond, will become the chief theatre of events in the world's great hereafter."

We need to remember this, especially in the State of Washington, which in some ways is more closely connected with the Orient than any other part of the country. That is why it has seemed necessary to preface what is here said with regard to Oriental immigration with a certain amount of generalization. The problem of immigration is a small one apart from its connection with the general problem of our national relations with China and Japan and the bearing of these relations upon the still larger question of world politics. As Darwin traced the failure of white clover in Australia to the killing of the cats which left the mice free to eat the bumble bees by means of which the clover was fertilized, so some small local prejudice against a Japanese laborer or storekeeper on the Pacific Coast may set in motion the machinery for a war embroiling the nations of two hemispheres.

With such portentous possibilities it is a real relief to confess that, so far as the State of Washington is concerned, there is no great cause for alarm. Whatever may be the temperature in British Columbia to the north and in California to the south, there is no hot blood, at the moment of writing, in Washington. Indeed, to some the discussion of the subject as a "problem" has seemed academic. A friend, speaking of the excited attempts of a very small group of exclusionists to rouse feeling on the subject, is reminded of poor Hood's pathetic remark, when they put the mustard plaster on his emaciated chest, "Don't you think there is a great deal of mustard to very little meat?" Twenty-five years ago there was considerable feeling as to Chinese immigration, the day of the Japanese was not yet, and riots took place in Seattle and Tacoma which have so far prevented any large Oriental migration to Tacoma. There are now no Chinese in that city and only 664 Japanese.

But there is little trace of the old bitterness. Here and there we have prejudice and dislike. Over-sensitive mothers fear an immoral influence from Orientals in school with their children. Exclusion leagues sporadically put forth their posters, "Fire the Japs," but the proceeding is half-hearted and suggests the need of the exclusionists themselves being "fired"—with enthusiam, if they are to make their cause a live issue. There can be little question that the general public sentiment of the State of Washington is fairly well expressed in a recent editorial of the "Post-Intelligencer" (Seattle), as follows:

"In an extensively advertised article by Mr. Will Irwin, of San Francisco, 'Pearson's Magazine,' printed in New York, undertakes to tell 'Why the Pacific Slope hates the Japanese.' The title of Mr. Irwin's article is rather too broad, for to undertake to explain 'why' the Japanese are 'hated,' is to assume hatred of the race as a fact, and that is error of a rather mischievous sort.

"It is obviously illogical to assume that because some Americans on this coast hate some Japanese, or because some Americans hate all Japanese, that, therefore, on this coast all Americans hate all Japanese.

"Mr. Irwin is perfectly competent to speak for that portion of San Francisco which has been under his immediate observation and study; but he is not authorized to speak for Washington, or for the city of Seattle.

"Washington is a part of the Pacific Slope; but so far as the vast majority of the men and women of this state are concerned, there is no hatred of the Japanese, no prejudice against the race, and no unkindly feeling for members of the race who now reside in this commonwealth. On their own account, they are perfectly welcome here.

"But aside from the inherent worth of good Japanese who have settled in this city and state, a vast majority of the people of Washington believe that these citizens of Japan should be accorded every right, privilege and immunity vouchsafed them in the solemn stipulations entered into by the United States government and the government of Japan.

"There may be Japanese problems in California; there is none here. There may be hatred of Japanese in California, but there is none here, and 'Pearson's' should be fairer and juster in its conclusions than to put Washington in a false attitude."

It is worth noticing, moreover, that during the recent visit to the Pacific Coast of the Japanese training squadron, under Vice-Admiral Ijichi, while in Vancouver, B. C., under the flag of Japan's ally, sufficient hostility was shown to prevent a parade of Japanese sailors under arms; in Seattle and Tacoma the welcome was of the warmest, and every appreciation of the sterling qualities of the Mikado's seamen was manifested.

Of course such a condition of feeling may not be permanent. Human nature is much the same in Washington as in California. Some sudden exacerbation of public sentiment might easily lead to hostile expression. But it is sufficiently evident that the hostility, wherever it may manifest itself, is not primarily *racial*. Dr. Josiah Royce has recently written:[1] "Our so-called race problems are merely the problems caused by our antipathies." Remembering this, we can see three or four reasons for the general absence in the State of Washington of antipathy towards the Orientals:

1. There is the consciousness that the immigration of Orientals is not now, nor is likely to be in the future, on such a scale as seriously to threaten the disturbance of the labor market. The number of Chinese now in the state is uncertain. In 1905 a census was commenced, but was not completed owing to the filing of protests from various quarters. So far as taken, I am informed by the inspector of immigration at this port, Mr. John H. Sargent, there were shown to be 2,936 Chinese in the state. Of this number 2,225 were laborers, 329 merchants, 264 natives of the state and 118 unclassified. Mr. Sargent believes the total number is less than 5,000 at the present time. The distribution, so far as the larger towns are concerned, is as follows: Seattle, 602; Spokane, 268; Walla Walla, 220; Blaine, 221; Anacortes, 218; Port Townsend, 160; Point Roberts, 146; Bellingham, 100. In the last named towns the Chinese are employed chiefly in the salmon canneries during the summer.

With regard to the Japanese, the figures furnished me by the Japanese Consulate are very explicit and show the Japanese population of 134 communities in the state. The total number is 9,056, a much smaller number than is popularly supposed. The distribution, mentioning again only the larger cities and towns, is as follows: Seattle, 3,134; Tacoma, 664; Spokane, 447; Bellingham, 150; Yakima, 149; Olympia, 57; Everett, 17. In some smaller places we have a larger proportion of Japanese, as, for instance, 403 at Fife, 74 at Walville, 75 at Leavenworth, 90 at Kerriston, 132 at Mukilteo, 103 at Littele, 96 at Startup. In these latter communities the presence of Japanese is due to local demands for labor in railway construction, canneries, logging camps, etc. In Seattle the bulk of the Japanese are engaged in mercantile pursuits, restaurants, hotels and in domestic service.

As to the immigration at present proceeding, we have an annual average of 700 Chinese entering the United States through the ports of this district. Of these the large majority are former residents of the United States. The new arrivals during the past year have not

[1] "Race Questions and Prejudices," p. 47.

exceeded fifty, and consist of "students, merchants, travelers for curiosity and pleasure, and officials of the Chinese Government."

With regard to the present rate of Japanese immigration I cannot do better than quote Mr. Sargent's words: "During the fiscal year ended June 30, 1908, approximately 4,500 Japanese entered the United States through ports of this state. Japanese immigration for the fiscal year ending June 30th, next (1909), will not exceed one-half of the above number." As Seattle is the principal port of entry for the Japanese who come to this country it will be seen that there is no great danger of our being overrun as things are at present. Passports, since the agreement of June, 1908, between the State Departments, are now issued to three classes of laborers only, viz., "former residents of the United States, parents or children of former residents and settled agriculturists." Not more than twenty-five have this past year been admitted as "settled agriculturists," *i. e.*, as those who own an interest in some farm or farming enterprise in the United States. A considerable proportion of the new arrivals are Japanese women who come to join the husbands to whom they have already been married in Japan by proxy. On their arrival they are now re-married according to the laws of the State of Washington.

2. There is no real fear, as matters stand, of any mischievous influence, morally and socially, through the presence of Orientals in the state. I may again quote from Mr. Sargent's letter to me: "At times in the past when complaints were raised by labor unions, exclusion leagues and others as to the number of Japanese arriving on this coast the department has sent our special officers to investigate. These officers on going aboard our boats found the Japanese to be young men, bright, active, intelligent, cleanly and well-dressed. On going ashore they found that none of them were in poor-houses or supported by charity." The presence of Japanese and Chinese in our schools and universities is not resented; they do good work and graduate with credit. There are now in the schools of Seattle, forty-seven Chinese (thirty-three boys and fourteen girls), and 242 Japanese (215 boys and twenty-seven girls). Nine Chinese and fifty Japanese are in high schools. Mr. F. B. Cooper, superintendent of schools, informs me: "Reports that come to me from the principals are that both the Japanese and Chinese are unobtrusive and studious, and that they occasion little or no difficulty so far as the administra-

tion of the school is concerned." He writes further, "we experience no difficulty whatever with either the Japanese or Chinese on moral grounds. They attend strictly to their own business, those that we have in school being newcomers to the country and knowing little or nothing of our language, keep naturally very much to themselves. The little children are tractable and apt." The state law does not, as in Oregon and California, forbid intermarriage between Japanese and whites and such marriages, while not frequent, are not unsuccessful, nor do they, except under extraordinary circumstances, attract any special attention.

The question of ultimate assimilation is one on which it is difficult to speak with any certainity. The Japanese themselves are to such an extent the result of fusion, combining such elements as Ainu, Mongol, Malay, Negrito, that a strain of white blood is not likely to diminish their vitality, whatever the Japanese strain may do for the Caucasian. It is quite certain as Dr. Gulick has shown in his "Evolution of the Japanese," that the differences between Japanese and Americans are not biological but sociological, due to environment rather than to unalterable physiological laws. At any rate, the Japanese element is too small to have an appreciable effect in altering the American type.

3. There is a very general conviction in Washington that the commercial interests of the Pacific Northwest demand close touch with the Orient and its peoples. With our present lack of a merchant marine, it is wise to encourage the commercial enterprise of the Chinese and Japanese. Their countrymen help to keep up and develop trade. Unfair treatment is apt to produce boycotts which are speedily felt by Pacific Coast merchants. Moreover, the standard of living in the Orient is raised by the example of Orientals who have had experience of life in American cities, and the raising of the standard of living in the Orient is the problem of the foreign merchant. It has been said with truth that to raise the standard of comfort in China by 50 per cent is to add commercially to the world's population 200 millions of human beings.

4. Beyond the merely negative sentiment of the causelessness for alarm and beyond the more or less selfish considerations of the business man there is growing up the sense of responsibility for harmonious international relations. The Oriental nations are no longer regarded as barbarians to be bullied at will. They have the

right, and the power to enforce the right, to be treated as self-respecting and honorable members of the great family of nations. It is felt, therefore, that the Oriental question must be regarded from a higher point of view than that of merely local and selfish interests. Of course, were the strain on our patience and good judgment suddenly intensified there is no telling what might happen, but at present there can be no doubt that our public men and the press are alive to the importance of looking at the Oriental problem from a national and even human point of view.

This much may be said by way of conclusion. In saying that there is little racial antipathy at present in Washington I have said less than the truth. On the positive side much is being done towards the creation of good relations. The Chamber of Commerce in Seattle has taken an active interest in promoting good feeling between the merchants of Japan and those of the state, sending and receiving delegations with accompaniments of the highest courtesy. The University of Washington is making a good beginning in providing for instruction in Oriental literature and languages. The churches, too, are active in the establishment of missions in the larger towns, and flourishing institutions conducted by six or seven religious bodies, exist in Seattle for the benefit of Japanese or Chinese.

Nor is this without result. Commerce is developed with the Orient itself through the presence of Oriental agents here. Education is advanced in Japan and China through the stimulus given by the graduates of American colleges. Moreover, religious work in China and Japan is wonderfully stimulated by the work accomplished amongst Orientals here. Bishop Restarick, of Honolulu has recently said that according to the testimony of Chinese and Japanese missionaries of long experience the converts in Hawaii, and the same is even truer of those on the Pacific Coast, are two or three generations ahead of the converts in the Orient itself. In such a gradual moral and intellectual assimilation of the members of alien races lies our best hope for the future. An iron-bound policy of exclusion can only keep apart, and that against the course of nature and against the interests of both sides of the Pacific. The fable of the clam, which boasted of its security from attack because of its ability to close its shell, and awoke to find itself on a fish-stall with the notice above it, "This clam, two cents," is as applicable to other countries as to Japan. Frank and honorable relations between the state departments of Oriental nations and our own, equally removed from doctrinaire sentimentalism and from pandering to popular prejudice; intelligent and humane administration of existing laws respecting immigrants; encouragement of the intercourse which shall promote mutual understanding and good will—these are the factors which will make the human more conspicuous than the racial and link together the two sides of the Pacific with the bonds of honorable and lasting peace.

THE EFFECT OF AMERICAN RESIDENCE ON JAPANESE

By BARON KENTARO KANEKO,
Tokio, Japan.

In 1873, Mr. Charles Flint, one of the school committee in Boston, stated to our Minister at Washington that Japanese students in America were studious and ambitious; that they were a credit to their own country, and at the same time gave a stimulus to American boys. They were then, he said, simply acorns, but would surely in the future become the oaks of national power in Japan. As predicted by the representative of the Boston School Committee, those Japanese have already become a part of the power which has made Japan what it is to-day!

However, some years ago there arose a question in Japan whether Japanese youths should not rather be sent to monarchial countries in Europe than to the United States, because the latter is a republic, where educational institutions and society are all founded upon democratic principles. It was claimed that Japanese might imbibe radical ideas, which, if not detrimental, are entirely foreign to the principle of our monarchial nation; but the result' of work by Japanese who returned from America showed that they were far more conservative than those educated in Europe. The men trained in America regularly gained the confidence of their superiors or employers. Consequently an American school certificate has been regarded as a strong recommendation for young men applying for any position in Japan, and they are welcomed in all the departments of government, as well as in business companies. To-day from the position of minister in the imperial cabinet down to managerships of private firms, the positions are nearly all filled by those who were one time resident in the United States.

Therefore it is often asked why an American education or sojourn has such an effect upon Japanese? To this I always answer that American life is full of energy and hope—energy stimulated by hope, and hope attained by work! Moreover, according to the psychology of the American people, man is taught to regard work as an end, and that to remain idle is a crime! To live in such an environment has a decidedly beneficial effect upon Japanese. Besides there is something in the American atmosphere which gives to a Japanese a new vigor as soon as he steps on American soil, and makes him ready to meet the fierce struggle of life. It makes no difference whether his stay in America be long or short, the Japanese holds fast to his bosom the feeling of gratitude toward America, which follows him even to the grave!

Many recent travelers after visiting Europe and America have said that Japanese who have been in America are earnest and active, and are the best qualified for any responsible position after they return home. The result of their work in Japan meets fully a parent's wishes; and now Japanese fathers are eager to send their sons and daughters to America, after they finish the studies at our colleges. Therefore the increase of Japanese in America has very great weight upon American influence in Japan, and a decrease will surely bring about a contrary result! Japanese in America have already served their country, doing credit to their American education, and thus doing honor to the United States. I hope sincerely that Japanese in America will in the future keep up the prestige already gained, and thereby recruit the American influence in Japan.

CHINESE LABOR COMPETITION ON THE PACIFIC COAST

By Mary Roberts Coolidge,
Formerly Associate Professor of Sociology, Stanford University, Cal.;
Author of "Chinese Immigration" (in press).

In discussing the question of Chinese competition in labor on the Pacific Coast it is ordinarily assumed that whenever a Chinaman enters any occupation he necessarily takes the place of an American or a European foreigner. But this does not at all correctly represent the true labor situation. The State of California, which contained three-fourths of the Chinese immigrants until after the exclusion law was passed, was settled by men drawn by the lure of gold, by adventurers and speculators of every class and nationality—industrial gamblers, in fact—who had no intention of earning a living there as laborers or domestics. They came to make no less than a fortune; and if they were driven to common tasks temporarily when their luck failed in mining or in the scarcely less hazardous business of provisioning camps and importing merchandise, they resented it and constituted, therefore, an exceptionally discontented and unstable laboring class. For almost a generation the stratum of society, which in any long-settled community is filled by those who cook, clean, wash and sew by those who perform the heavy, drudging labor fundamental to industrial development, was all but lacking. There were almost no women or youth who would work even at exorbitant wages, and until the Kearney period no considerable supply of common laborers. At times the vacuum was partially filled by those newly-arrived or down on their luck, but all of them would desert at the news of a new gold-strike or at the chance of any sort of promising speculation.

The Chinese laborers, therefore, coming almost exclusively from the free agricultural peasantry of Kwang Tung and Fukien, were welcome, and, being more enticed by the tales of high wages than by the golden adventure, fitted naturally into the labor vacuum left by men of more adventurous disposition. They became—what they still remain for the most part—gap-fillers—assuming the menial, petty and laborious work which white men would not do and for which their experience and their native characteristics especially prepared them.

The question has, furthermore, generally been discussed with reference to conditions existing in a few towns and the one large city, San Francisco; yet, during three decades of free immigration, a majority of the Chinamen were in the rural and mountain districts engaged in domestic, agricultural and general labor and in placer mining. In these sparsely populated and often very remote regions their services were acknowledged to be indispensable and only partly filled a demand which has never been supplied by native or foreign workers. Even in placer mining they worked chiefly the poor and abandoned claims which white men left untouched and rarely attempted to compete for the higher prizes of fortune.

During the first twenty years of California history there were, indeed, occasional anti-Chinese movements coincident with political campaigns, when candidates and agitators catered to the mining vote by appeals to a natural race antipathy which had been intensified by the reconstruction measures after the Civil War. But the objection to the Chinese in the earlier time was a phase of the initial struggle of the Americans against all foreigners for the control of the mines; and somewhat later took the form of a general apprehension of "an invasion of heathen hordes" rather than complaint of the competition of Oriental labor. Without rehearsing in detail the proofs, it may be stated finally that at this period the Chinese were a considerable and indispensable element in California progress and in no proper sense competitors of white labor. Even Mr. Samuel Gompers has granted that up to 1869 the presence of the Chinese "caused no serious alarm or discomfort to white labor."

But within the decade following the opening of the Central Pacific Railway the industrial conditions of the Far West were rapidly altered. The builders of the Southern Pacific, after employing every available white laborer at good wages, had been compelled to prepay the passages of thousands of Chinese immigrants in order to finish the road within the time required by Congress; and upon its completion ten thousand whites and Chinese were discharged upon the western labor market. Shortly afterward the greater ease of travel, the phenomenal mining stock sales and two successive years of abundant rainfall upon which mining and agricultural prosperity depended, greatly stimulated immigration from the eastern states. In 1868 and 1869 there came into the state 59,000 white immigrants—a number more than double the net increase of the ten years previous. The railway, instead of bringing in a general era of prosperity, as had been anticipated, opened California markets to eastern competition and at once reduced profits on local manufactures and commodities, while immigration precipitated the inevitable fall of wages, which had remained extraordinarily high as a consequence of isolation and the conditions of pioneer mining. Before western society had become readjusted to these disconcerting results of closer union with the world the panic of 1873 struck the eastern states and settled into a prolonged depression. The financial status of California, being established on a gold basis and chiefly supported by the mines, was not at first adversely or directly affected; but indirectly she began to share the disaster through the thousands of unemployed who had come from the stagnation of eastern cities to the land where gold and work were said to be still abundant.

Unfortunately, the white migrants were of a class of which the state already had an over-supply: factory workers, clerks, semi-skilled artisans, and men of low-grade city occupations. The records of the California Labor Exchange, which handled the greater part of the unemployed in San Francisco from 1868 to 1870, show that even in those thriving years there was an excessive supply of waiters, painters, dishwashers, grooms, porters, bookkeepers, salesmen. warehousemen and indoor workmen of all kinds, while there was an unfilled demand for heavy labor on construction works and farms, for lumbermen and machine blacksmiths, and for women and boys as cooks and helpers. Fifty per cent of the applicants were Irish, ten per cent English and Scotch, ten per cent German and only nineteen per cent native American, of whom a considerable number must have been of Irish or German parentage. The labor market continued to be recruited from men of no use in the country and most of whom would not go there even at wages much above those to which they had been accustomed.

About 1874 the inevitable fall of wages, so long postponed by abnormal conditions, began. Measured by the eastern standard, they were still high throughout the whole Kearney period. From the California standpoint they were falling terribly; and to the workingmen they seemed to threaten a less than living wage. In cooking,

sewing and laundry work they remained through the seventies practically stationary at three times the average eastern rate. In farm
labor, though falling slowly, they averaged 33 per cent above the
Middle West; while in those "services on the spot," which are slow
to feel the effects of competition, they remained permanently far
above the standard of older communities. The accompanying table,
covering nineteen trades between 1870 and 1890, demonstrates the
superiority of San Francisco conditions during the national depression:

COMPARISON OF MAXIMUM AND MINIMUM DAILY WAGES OF NINETEEN TRADES
IN SAN FRANCISCO AND IN ELEVEN OTHER CITIES, 1870-1890.[1]

TRADE.	Max. 11 cities.	Min. 11 cities.	Range in cents.	Max. S. F.	Min. S. F.	Range in cents.	Amt. by which min. of S. F. exceeds max. of 11 cities.
Blacksmiths	$2.70	$2.43	$0.27	$3.80	$3.33	$0.47	$0.63
Blacksmith's helpers ...	1.59	1.41	.18	2.34	2.09	.25	.50
Boiler makers	2.69	2.41	.28	3.46	3.15	.31	.46
Bricklayers	4.13	3.00	1.13	5.00	4.00	1.00	.13
Carpenters	2.60	2.28	.32	3.85	3.09	.76	.49
Compositors	2.82	2.64	.18	3.54	3.27	.27	.45
Engineers (R. R.)	4.02	3.49	.53	4.79	4.53	.26	.51
Firemen (R. R.)	2.03	1.75	.28	3.06	2.54	.52	.51
Hod carriers	2.20	1.58	.62	3.00	2.35	.65	.15
Iron molders	2.79	2.36	.43	3.71	3.40	.31	.61
Laborers (street)	1.63	1.45	.18	2.50	2.00	.50	.37
Laborers (general)	1.57	1.40	.17	2.00	1.97	.03	.40
Machinists	2.52	2.22	.30	3.36	2.95	.41	.43
Masons (stone)	3.62	2.81	.81	5.00	4.83	.17	.21
Painters	2.66	2.16	.50	3.72	3.00	.72	.34
Pattern makers	2.98	2.68	.30	3.89	3.15	.74	.17
Plumbers	3.15	2.79	.36	3.69	3.55	.14	.40
Stone cutters	3.64	2.66	.98	4.11	3.66	.45	.02
Teamsters	1.95	1.71	.25	2.67	2.62	.05	.67
Averages	$2.69	$2.27	$0.42	$3.55	$3.13	$0.89	$0.39

It appears that during twenty years the minimum average wage
in San Francisco in eighteen of nineteen trades exceeded the maxi-

[1] Reprinted from Coolidge, *Chinese Immigration* (in press).
Bul. 18, U. S. Dept. of Labor, 1898. Rearranged.

mum average wage in eleven other cities, the total average excess amounting to thirty-nine cents per day per trade. Nor was this excess diminished by an appreciable difference in the cost of living.

Nevertheless, during this very period there occurred the labor outbreak known as Kearneyism, whose animus was concentrated upon the rich, monopolistic corporations and upon the Chinese. The movement was in fact a reflection of the wider national labor agitation, and had its origin in a network of local industrial grievances. The demand for labor was erratic and its conditions unstable. When the eastern depression finally made itself felt in California the check upon industry was intensified by drought, and to the thousands of eastern unemployed were added more than the normal number of those who in the West are usually out of work from December to March. A large number of the immigrants were such as could not have found work in California even in prosperous times, and a study of the principal industries suggests that the situation was greatly aggravated by the extremely intermittent character of all rural employments. As the rainy season came on the placer miners, both white and Chinese, returned to the valley towns and to the coast. Farm laborers had work only from March to July or August and a few for the short plowing season in early winter, after which they, too, drifted into San Francisco. All the industries dependent on mining and farming suffered the same seasonal contraction. The failure of winter rainfall, just before the Kearney, uprising, resulted in widespread unemployment and consequent congestion of workers in San Francisco. Then, as now, during the winter months, certain streets were thronged with idle and disgruntled men, among whom the agitator and the demagogue found ready listeners. Chinatown as well was filled up with miners, fishermen and laborers, to whom were added in February and March the usual quota of spring immigrants from Hongkong. Men are not logical when their wages are falling or when they are unemployed— the mere juxtaposition of thousands of both races, even though many of them would find abundant and well-paid work in the country at the opening of the next spring, made it seem evident that there must be intense competition. Yet the recurring congestion and lack of work was due to climatic and economic conditions with which the Chinamen had nothing to do.

During the seventies the Chinese had been gradually shifting from the mining to the agricultural and urban counties, until, in 1880, about one-third of the whole number were in towns, and from 20,000 to 25,000 in San Francisco at various seasons. It has been shown that if there was competition anywhere, it was in manufacture, and in the principal city where such factory industries as there were chiefly existed. In a pamphlet entitled "Meat *vs.* Rice," published by the American Federation of Labor, eight industries are specifically mentioned as the most important of those from which the Chinese had driven white labor. Only three of them, however, employed Chinamen in any considerable numbers and turned out sufficient product to merit any examination. The boot and shoe industry, the woolen industry and cigar-making are the manufactures frequently named in anti-Chinese literature as unquestionable examples of severe competition, and should, therefore, be individually studied.

In the boot and shoe industry there were engaged in the seventies from 1,500 to 2,500 persons, of whom 26 per cent were Irish, 21 per cent Americans and 19 per cent each Germans and Chinese. The competition, it is evident, must have been between the Irish and German foreigners on the one hand and the Oriental foreigners on the other, if, as is usual, the overseers and foremen were Americans. This manufacture, begun as the result of the superior quality of hides and leather in California, suffered a sudden check upon the finishing of the railway because of the opening of the home market to eastern producers. Although leather was relatively cheap, it was shipped east, manufactured and shipped back, and sold at a greater profit than could be made on home manufactured goods. From two-thirds to three-fourths of the goods manufactured by the Chinese in San Francisco were made in Chinese shops and sold to their countrymen, the product being principally coarse boots and shoes for laborers and cheap slippers. It was said that they never could make fine footwear, but it may be that they, too, found competition with eastern-made goods unprofitable. The Knights of Saint Crispin, a union of shoemakers newly organized in the West, demanded that the manufacturers employ white labor; but when, under the intimidation of Kearneyism, the substitution was agreed to, it was found necessary to send east for operatives. Nor did wages ever fall to the eastern level except in those operations where the Chinese took the places of the women and children so largely employed in eastern factories after the introduction of shoe machinery. It is clear that a local industry, 48 per cent of whose operatives in the east were women, must have had some considerable advantages to maintain itself. As a matter of fact, California had only a cheaper raw material and Chinese labor—which was paid about the same as women elsewhere—to oppose to the · generally cheaper labor and much cheaper fuel and capital of eastern producers. Even with its local advantages the industry throve only for a short time, and the Chinese manufacture in Chinese shops declined as rapidly as the American. In 1870 this industry ranked fourth in the state; by 1893 its production had declined to less than half what it had been, and at present it has not even a place among the sixteen leading industries.

The woolen industry has a similar history. Established in 1867 by a Scotchman because of the superiority of California wool, it employed at its height about 1,000 operatives. It was never able to compete with the eastern product in certain lines and in the others only paid dividends after the Chinese began to be employed. California was employing only one woman and one youth to nineteen men (both white and Chinese), while the other states were employing in this manufacture one woman and one child to every two to five men. A comparison of the wages of different classes of employees, from 1867 to 1880, in the East and the Far West shows that the total average wage of the eight classes in which Chinese were engaged was exactly the same as of the same classes in seven other states; while the average of nine other classes in which white men were employed was one dollar per day higher in California than elsewhere. Even with Chinese labor the wages of California woolen factories never reached the lower level of the East. Between 1880 and 1890 the industry began to decline, the number employed fell from 819 to 125, and its product dwindled from $1,700,000 to $350,000.

The third trade, cigar-making, in which the Chinese are said to have superseded Americans has had almost as disastrous a history. Established in the West by Germans, in 1870 it was employing from 2,000 to 2,500 persons and a few years later perhaps twice as many. It had fallen almost wholly into the hands of the Chinese and the scale of wages was about ten per cent less than those of eastern and southern establishments. In 1877 the statistics of seventeen white firms in San Francisco, most of them German, show a total of 263 Chinese earning $2.75 per day; and 133 more $3.00 per day;

while 2,800 Chinese were employed by Chinese manufacturers at fifty cents to $1.25 per day and board. In 1878, at the demand of the White Labor League, most of the white firms agreed to replace all Chinese with white labor at union wages in order to give the unemployed work. It was at once disclosed that there were very few cigar makers out of work in San Francisco and the unions sent East for several hundred men, many of whom ultimately returned to the East or left the trade for more alluring occupations in California. In spite of the gradual re-engagement of many Chinese the industry rapidly declined, owing, it is said, to the severe competition of Eastern tenement-house and Cuban labor. As in the case of the shoe industry, the Chinese manufacture also declined, and in 1891, the Hong Tuck Tong—Chinese Cigar Makers' Union—had only one-fourth as many members as formerly.

The history of these three factory industries in which the Chinese were largely employed, and of many small ones, shows that, except in cigar-making, wages did not reach the level of Eastern manufacture. The relatively low wages in them were probably due to the narrow margin of profit and to the impossibility of permanent success under local conditions. It does not appear that any number of white men were displaced by Chinese; but undoubtedly the presence of a large number of white immigrants unfitted for California occupations, as well as of Chinese who could be had more cheaply, hastened the fall of wages from the pioneer standard to a level approaching that of the rest of the country. Yet without the Chinese some of these manufactures would not have survived at all. If it be contended that white men were driven to accept "Chinese wages" still the inexorable fact of Eastern competition has to be reckoned with. The unanswerable fact is that whereas these three manufactures once ranked among the leading ones of the state, their combined product in 1906 was not as much as that of one of its sixteen principal industries. If the Chinese excluded white labor from them originally then it may now be argued that the exclusion of the Chinese has killed the industries. But neither hypothesis can be sustained; rather we must suppose that certain kinds of manufacture in California were premature and their decline due to causes only remotely connected with the labor supply.

One other contention—that the Chinese took the places of women and boys—may be briefly considered, although it scarcely seems to require demonstration that in a region where there were, even in 1880, only three females to five males of all races; and only one child of school age to every three or four adults, such women and youth as wished to work could not fail to find work when there was work for anyone. During the Kearney period women constituted less than six per cent of the total number in gainful occupations; and about fifty per cent of those in the sewing trades in which the Chinese were ten per cent. The wages of women in every line of household labor and in the sewing trades were and have remained far higher than anywhere else in the United States. It is true that Chinamen performed a large part of the domestic labor in California, but always at wages higher than those of women and with an ever-rising demand, until at present a Chinese cook is a luxury that only the rich can afford.

In the discussion of Chinese labor competition only two conspicuous qualities of the Chinese laborer himself are commonly mentioned: his thrift and his laborious patience; yet he has several other characteristics of even greater pertinence to the question. Free Chinese labor never remains "cheap" for any great length of time. In California the Chinamen are receiving on the average twice as much in wages as in 1882 and more than similar classes of naturalized Europeans. They are not only organized more thoroughly and minutely into unions than Americans but they have an adaptability and a keenness which enable them to distribute themselves quickly to the districts and the occupations where competition is least and wages highest. They have left factory labor and washing because wages were too low, although the Chinese laundrymen are paying twice the wages they paid twenty years ago. In fact among the fifty or sixty thousand remaining in California, most of whom were originally laborers, a majority are now the owners of small independent businesses or employed in coöperative undertakings. In Hawaii, where the Chinese are preferred to any other class of common labor, it is the complaint that the Chinameh will not remain laborers and now expect to make white men's profits in their business enterprises.

Again, it is a mistake to suppose that the Chinaman lives penuriously on rice and wholly without meat. He does, indeed, live within his income, but, because of his industry, intelligent ambition and thrift, he generally has money in his pocket, and no man likes to spend it for good food and for pleasures more than he. Professor Jaffa has concluded from an exhaustive study of the dietaries of three groups of Chinese—washmen, truck-gardeners and students,— that their food is quite as nutritious and more varied than that of white workingmen, small tradesmen and farm-hands in the same region. The somewhat lower cost he attributes to less wasteful habits and greater skill in preparation, on the part of the Orientals. The ability to cook, sew and wash for himself, as the white laborer can seldom do satisfactorily, is also a considerable advantage both to the employer and to the Chinaman in the homeless life he leads. His native thrift and his moderation both in his pleasures and his vices enable him to endure with less danger of degeneration the effects of intermittent employment.

The enumeration of the Chinese laborer's industrial virtues would seem to render him a dangerous competitor of the white laborer, but as a matter of fact he never became one, except to an infinitesimal degree in California, partly because of the lack of any other distinct laboring class in number sufficient to supply the ever-increasing demand, and partly because of the intelligent ambition of the Chinaman himself, which soon took him out of the laboring class. Certain personal characteristics also prevented him from attempting competition in lines where aggressiveness was required. The Chinaman, though keen and industrious and saving, is timid and conservative, intelligently preferring moderate wages in peace to a job which he must fight for. He is usually a married man with a wife and parents in China, to whom he will be devoted throughout the enforced absence of years and to whom he will return as soon as he has saved enough capital to insure a comfortable business at home. When he remains here and brings over a wife, he may not lose his native characteristics, but he will try to raise his children by education into a higher class and insist upon making good Americans of them.

From the time of the Scott act (1888), when the Chinese laborers in California began to decline perceptibly in numbers, there have been many attempts to fill their places. Except immediately after the panic of 1893, there has been a temporary and in some localities a permanent "labor famine" every season, while wages have been rising. The substitutes for the vanishing Chinamen are vari-colored—Negroes, Apache and Yaqui Indians, Mexicans and

Cholos, Italians, Greeks, Austrians and Portuguese, Hawaiians and Hindoos, Porto Ricans, Filipinos, and lastly Japanese. Since the work of California must be done somehow and by someone, it may be questioned whether the dangers of Chinese competition in labor are greater than those likely to be encountered from most of these other races, whose assimilative power is even less than that of the Chinaman, and who certainly have far less industrial efficiency.

THE LEGISLATIVE HISTORY OF EXCLUSION LEGISLATION

By Chester Lloyd Jones, Ph.D.,
Intructor in Political Science, University of Pennsylvania, Philadelphia.

The laws passed in various countries restricting Oriental immigration are of two classes, relating to coolie labor and regulating the general immigration of Oriental races. Experiments with coolie labor have been made under many conditions and satisfactory results have often been obtained, especially in tropical countries, where the white man cannot do heavy work. But in the temperate zones the presence of the coolie is always unwelcome to the white laborer, whom he undersells, and if provision is not made for his return to his native country at the end of his labor term he soon becomes quite as objectionable to the white employer as to the laboring classes. His economic advantages soon enable him to leave the rough work for which he was engaged and to push his way through artisanship to commerce and manufacture. When that occurs the upper classes of the dominant race begin to see their own field encroached upon and the legislation becomes of the second class— that directed against the general immigration of Oriental races.[1]

Through this development the United States has passed, for though nominally we have prohibited coolie labor since the days of the Burlingame treaty, it must be admitted that through much of the time the employment of Chinese was under the control of contractors who only veiled the conditions of employment in such a way as to avoid the terms of the treaty. Then as the Chinese who had served their terms and those who came of their own free will entered the various occupations, the laborers and at last the whole west coast population, cried out for general exclusion, which now they would have extended to cover Japanese, Koreans and even the Aryan Hindoo, as well as the despised Chinaman.

The immigration from China—the first to start from the Orient —in the beginning caused no comment. It grew but slowly. In the

[1] See discussion of Oriental Labor in South Africa, elsewhere in this volume. Peru is going through the same experience. A decree was issued May 14, 1909, suspending Chinese immigration pending action by the Congress.

period 1820-40 there were but eleven arrivals; the next twelve years brought but thirty-five. In 1854 came the first notable increase, 13,110 entering California in that year. Locally prejudice began to crystallize against the newcomers, but the government at Washington was complacent in the belief that no fear was justified, for the Chinese came only to earn money and return, seldom bringing their wives. It regarded "adverse legislation" as "not at all likely."[1] There was, up to 1870, only an occasional entry from Japan. The Secretary of Agriculture favored Orientals for rough work, they "would really operate only as labor-saving machinery does."[2] The Burlingame treaty was adopted in 1869 with no protest. It was still felt that a regulation of coolie labor was all that was necessary.

California, however, was soon convinced that restriction was needed. On December 22, 1869, an unsuccessful effort was made to secure action by Congress.[3] In 1872 the legislature instructed the representatives in Congress to urge the making of a treaty which should discourage Chinese immigration.[4] Similar action was taken two years later.[5] Congress finally appointed a joint special committee to investigate Chinese immigration in the summer of 1876. The committee, in its report of over 1,200 pages, reached no definite recommendations, though the tone of the report was anti-Chinese. The evidence was confused and conflicting. California was held to have advanced more rapidly through the presence of the Chinese, they were found to live in unsanitary quarters, and their "many young children," were provided with no education.[6]

From this time on protest and defense became continuous. The legislature of California in 1877 protested to Congress against the social, moral and political effect of Chinese immigration.[7] The male adults almost equaled the voting population of the state. "No nation, much less a republic, can safely permit the presence of a large and increasing element among its people which cannot be assimilated." On the other hand, the congressional committee's re-

[1] House Exec. Doc., 3d Sess., 41st Cong., Vol. 13, pp. 572-6.
[2] Ibid.
[3] See House Report, 45th Cong., 3d Sess., No. 62.
[4] House Misc. Doc., 42d Cong., 2d Sess., No. 120.
[5] House Misc. Doc., 43d Cong., 1st Sess., 204. See also protest from Beaver County, Pa., against the importation of 165 Chinese by a cutlery company. House Misc. Doc., 42d Cong., 3d Sess., No. 181.
[6] Senate Report, 44th Congress, 2d Sess., No. 689.
[7] House Misc. Doc., 45th Cong., 1st Sess., No. 9.

part is impugned as *ex parte* and largely mistaken.[9] The Chinese are
defended for the work they did which made the transcontinental
roads possible and for the draining of over a million acres of tule
lands in California, which, without them, would have remained
waste.[10] It is pointed out that in California the Chinese pay school
taxes, but they are excluded from the schools—only one little girl
out of over 3,000 was studying in a public school. In Congress bills
were introduced for placing a head tax of $250.00 on each Chinese
immigrant and making evasion of the tax a crime punishable by
five years' hard labor in the state prison.[11] The legislature in 1878
again appealed to Congress for relief,[12] and a house committee reported that China "was separated from us by a comparatively narrow
ocean," the rates on which had by competition fallen from fifty
dollars to twelve; that as a result the Chinese worked on the Pacific
Coast for from twenty to thirty cents a day, slept in crowded quarters "like sardines in a box" and were unassimilable, and, therefore,
undesirable as an element of our population.[13] China, it is asserted,
does not favor emigration, hence there is no fear of international
difficulty. "But were it otherwise the harmony and perpetuity of our
social and political institutions" could not be weighed against any
advantage of Chinese commerce. Thus early was the importance
of keeping California "a white man's country" an impelling motive
in the movement for restriction urged by these repeated appeals.

Congress finally decided not to wait longer for action by the
treaty power. "So long a period of non-action proved either the
non-willingness or the inability of the treaty-making power to cope
with the question. . . . This whole question is not one of right,
but one of policy.[14] The house passed a bill limiting the number of
passengers which might be brought by any one vessel to fifteen.
The senate amended by stipulating for abrogation of two articles
of our treaty with China. President Hayes vetoed this bill because
it would force us to break the faith of a treaty—and would expose
our citizens in China to retaliation. He believed that a modification
of the treaty would be willingly assented to by China.[16] Accord-

[9]Senate Misc. Doc., 2d Sess., 45th Cong., No. 20.
[10]*Ibid.*
[11]Senate Misc. Doc., 2d Sess., 45th Cong., No. 20.
[12]House Misc. Doc., 45th Cong., 2d Sess., No. 20, February 4, 1878.
[13]House Report, 45th Cong., 2d Sess., No. 240, February 25, 1878.
[14]House Report. 45th Cong., 3d Sess., No. 62.
[16]House Exec. Doc., 45th Cong., 3d Sess., No. 102, March 10, 1879.

ingly, the following year negotiations for change of the treaty were undertaken.[16] Meanwhile California had submitted the question of exclusion to a popular vote. The result indicates the popular feeling. Within 4,000 of the entire state vote was cast, of which number 154,638 votes were against and 883 in favor of Chinese immigration. "The result of such a verdict comes up to the American Congress with a degree of force that cannot safely be resisted," reported the select committee charged with investigating the causes for the existing depression of labor in 1880. So important apparently did they think this question that their report deals only with Chinese immigration, though the instructions were to investigate all reasons for the depression of the labor market. The discussion presented, though prejudiced throughout, gives a good idea of the state of public opinion at the time in the coast states—from which came the majority of the members of the committee.[17] "The Sierra Nevadas now mark the pagan boundary. Let us make a solemn decree that beyond that high boundary the invading swarm must stop."[18]

The treaty of November 5, 1881, aimed to stop this ill feeling by providing that the United States might "regulate, limit or suspend" "the coming of Chinese laborers . . . but (might) not absolutely prohibit it." Congress was in a spirit to exercise the maximum of the power thus granted and passed a bill suspending immigration for twenty-five years. Like its predecessors, the measure was vetoed. President Arthur declared neither party contemplated a prohibition of so long a term. He stated in his message to Congress, "I regard this provision of the act as a breach of our national faith."[19] The bill failed to pass over the veto,[20] and at once other bills providing for ten, sixteen and twenty-year periods of exclusion were introduced. Finally a compromise between the legislature and the executive was reached in the bill approved May 6, 1882. It was a measure framed by the representatives of the three states and two territories most affected, "all the talent of the Pacific Coast (being) enlisted in its drafting."[21] The immigration of Chi-

[16]House Exec. Doc., 46th Cong., 2d Sess., No. 70.
[17]House Report, 46th Cong., 2d Sess., No. 572, March 19, 1880.
[18]Ibid.
[19]Senate Exec. Doc., 47th Cong., 1st Sess., No. 148, April 4, 1882. See also House Report, 47th Cong., 1st Sess., No. 67, January 26, 1882; House Report, 47th Cong., 1st Sess., No. 1017, April 12, 1882.
[20]House Report, 47th Cong., 1st Sess., No. 1017, Part II, April 14, 1882.
[21]House Report, 48th Cong., 1st Sess., No. 614, March 4, 1884.

nese laborers was suspended for ten years, except of such as were in the United States November 17, 1880, or should come within ninety days after the passage of the bill. Those lawfully in the United States could return to China without losing the right of entry here by taking out a "return certificate" at the port in the United States whence they sailed. Great difficulty at once arose in administering the law, some of its provisions could not be executed, others were easy of evasion and in some cases there was great corruption in the sale by the immigration officers of certificates entitling a man to return to the United States.[22] Minor amendments to the law were added July 5, 1884.

From the first this law did not satisfy the West, which had had a free hand in its framing. In March, 1886, an anti-Chinese state convention was held in Sacramento to memorialize Congress in favor of absolute prohibition.[23] Numerous riots due to race prejudice occurred in all the western states.[24] At Rock Springs, Wyoming, a night attack by 150 armed men was made upon the Chinese, their houses were plundered and then burned, the Chinese were pursued and shot "like a herd of antelopes, making no resistance." In many towns in California they were driven out, sometimes without notice, in other cases after warning; at some seaports they were forced on board boats returning to China. The local authorities regularly refused to interfere to prevent or punish abuse of the Orientals. President Cleveland, in a message asking Congress to pay damages as an act of friendship, a suggestion later acted upon, asserted that "the proceedings in the name of justice for the ascertainment of the crime and fixing the responsibility therefor were a ghastly mockery of justice."

Such conditions were not to be borne. In 1886 China undertook to prohibit the coming of laborers to this country and later agreed to a treaty which would allow the United States a free hand in the matter. In the expectation that his agreement would be ratified, Congress undertook thoroughgoing exclusion legislation. At the last moment, however, China took action which was held to indicate a desire to block the negotiations indefinitely.[25] On that account

---

[22] See especially House Exec. Doc., 48th Cong., 2d Sess., No. 214.
[23] Senate Misc. Doc., 49th Cong., 1st Sess., No. 107, April 28, 1886.
[24] House Exec. Doc., 49th Cong., 1st Sess., 102. Message of President Cleveland gives numerous instances.
[25] Senate Exec. Doc., 50th Cong., 1st Sess., No. 273.

President Cleveland decided to approve the bill which had been intended to be supplemental to the treaty, alleging that the United States was called upon "to act in advance by the exercise of its legislative power."[26]

The act of 1888 excluded all Chinese except certain classes, such as officials, teachers, merchants or travelers. Even such could come only after getting permission of the home government and an identification slip issued by the consular representatives of the United States at the port of sailing. Chinese laborers already in this country, except if they had a family or property worth $1,000, could not return if they left the United States. Those having these qualifications could return within one year upon producing the return certificates which it was provided should be issued at their departure. This law, like that of 1882, was evaded. Fraudulent certificates, smuggling across the borders of Canada and Mexico, and abuse of transit privileges were alleged as the most frequent abuses.[27]   To meet this difficulty Congress at once took up measures for the enumeration of all Chinese in the country and providing that all not having certificates should be deported.[28]

No law on this subject was passed, however, until 1892. The exclusion proper rested on the act of 1882, which, by the ten-year limitation, was then soon to go out of force. To avoid this possibility the Geary act was passed, continuing in force all anti-Chinese legislation for another decade. The changes which had been urged were also incorporated. It was provided that all Chinese must have certificates to prove their right to remain. If any were found illegally within the United States they were to be deported, unless some good reason for not having procured the certificate was shown and actual residence at the time the law was passed could be proven by at least one witness other than Chinese.[29]

The Chinese employed counsel—among whom was Hon. Rufus Choate—to contest the constitutionality of this law. By advice they did not register, and when the court had rendered its decision up-

[26]Act of September 13, 1888, c. 1015, 25 Stat. 476; see also act of October 1, 1888, c. 1064, 25 Stat. 504.
[27]Senate Exec. Doc., 51 Cong., 1st Sess., No. 97.
[28]Senate Exec. Doc., 51st Cong., 1st Sess., No. 106; Senate Misc. Doc., 51st Cong., 1st Sess., No. 123, April 9, 1890; House Report, 51st Congress, 1st Session, No. 486, February 27, 1890; House Report, 51st Cong., 1st Sess., No. 2915, and House Report, 51st Cong., 2d Sess., No. 4078.
[29]Act of May 5, 1892, c. 60, 27 Stat. 25. See House Exec. Doc., 52d Cong., 1st Sess., No. 224.

holding the law the time for registering was passed. All were, therefore, technically liable to deportation; so, to relieve this situation, Congress extended the registration period for six months. Additional rules were also provided, and to aid identification it was required that the return certificates be accompanied by a photograph of the recipient.[30]

The following year a new treaty with China embodied practically the items of the Geary act and abolished the provision of the act of 1888, by which laborers leaving the United States were denied the privilege of return. It was to last for ten years, at the end of which time, in 1904, China declined to renew it. In the meantime Hawaii had been annexed and the exclusion laws were extended to that territory by the "act to provide a government for the territory," approved April 30, 1900.[31] The second period for which the exclusion act of 1882 was being enforced had also come to an end. As that time approached interest in the exclusion laws had again become intense on the Pacific Coast, especially under the lead of the American Federation of Labor.[32] Typical of public opinion also was a convention held in San Francisco November 21, 1901, composed of state, county and city officers and representatives of trade organizations to the number of 3,000. It voted unanimously for exclusion.[33] The Chinese minister, on the other hand, exerted his influence through the Department of State in opposition to the re-enactment of the discriminating legislation.[34] The minister particularly objected to the harsh administration of the laws by the Treasury Department, especially since 1898. He showed that the act was originally aimed at laborers only, but that the government now excluded every one not specifically named in the exempt classes, including even bankers, physicians and other classes, against whom the law was never intended to act. A protest against the inclusion of Hawaii was made on the ground that it could never be a field for exploitation by Anglo-Saxon laborers. A similar objection was raised to the act of General Otis in extending the exclusion acts to the Philippines.

[30] House Report, 53d Cong., 1st Sess., No. 7, October 4, 1893; Act of November 3, 1893, c. 14, 28 Stat. 7.
[31] Senate Report, 55th Cong., 3d Sess., No. 1654, February 13, 1899. See also U. S. Statutes, 1897-8, p. 751, and House Doc., 56th Cong., 2d Sess., No. 464.
[32] Senate Doc., 57th Cong., 1st Sess., No. 137.
[33] Senate Doc., 57th Cong., 1st Sess., No. 191.
[34] Senate Doc., 57th Cong., 1st Sess., No. 162.

But the country had by this time become accustomed to the exclusion acts and Congress was satisfied with their principle. There was no difficulty in inducing the legislature to accede to the demand for the indefinite extension of the life of the laws by the act of April 22, 1902.[38] This law expressly extended the legislation to all the island territories and prohibited the emigration of Chinese from them to the continental United States or from islands to other islands not of the same group. In fact, this rule had been applied in the Philippines since an order issued by General Otis in September, 1899. Certificates of residence were also required in the insular possessions.

This law is the last important one affecting Chinese immigration. The general policy indicated by the various acts is, judging from the present state of public opinion, not likely soon to undergo further important change. Such modifications as have been introduced during the last seven years have been in the direction of making the administration of the laws stricter and toward a narrower construction of the meaning to be placed upon the words describing the privileged classes.

The reasons for this condition are of two sorts. The people at large, now that a saner attitude toward all our racial questions is developing, are less to be aroused by appeals to abstract equal rights. The presence of elements not easily assimilable among our population has made the public look askance at any action which may introduce another element that may complicate the problem of adjustment. In the Far West the subject is of course a local one and correspondingly acute. There the appeal to keep California a "white man's country" has a greater immediate force on public opinion. Exclusion is there anything but an academic question. In the East, due to the small number of Orientals in the laboring population, interest is less lively. It is an indication of increasing class consciousness that in both sections of the country the laboring classes are the most alive to what Oriental labor means for the white man. Their interests are the ones which will be affected first. For these reasons we can probably look forward to a long period during which our legislation on Oriental immigration will undergo but slight change—unless it be in the direction of further restriction and the inclusion of other races besides the Chinese. That such a development may occur or is perhaps in process is clearly

[38] Act of April 22, 1902, c. 641, 32 Stat. 176.

indicated by the recent agitation on the coast to make the exclusion laws apply to all Oriental immigrants.

For the present an agreement has been reached which may put off or remove altogether the possibility of legislation against Japanese laborers. Japan, like China before her, professedly does not want her emigrants to go to the United States. The desire to get a preponderant influence in Korea and perhaps in Manchuria prompts the government to turn thither all those who leave the home country. Indeed, for some time past it has been the custom of Japan not to issue passports to laborers desiring to go to the United States, but since no restriction was placed on emigration to Hawaii, Canada and Mexico, the regulation was ineffective.

The agitation on the Pacific Coast, which became acute in 1906, forced the attention of Congress to the fact that legislation similar to that in force against the Chinese was being demanded for Japanese immigrants. The excitement was for the time at least allayed by an expedient included in the immigration act of 1907. Placing reliance on the continuation of Japan's policy as regards emigration noted above, Congress authorized the President to exclude from continental United States any immigrants holding passports not specifically entitling them to enter this country. On March 14, 1907, the President exercised this right by an executive order applying to Japanese laborers coming from Mexico, Canada or Hawaii.[96]

Due to this arrangement, the local legislation which caused the excitement was withdrawn, and the "Japanese question" was for the moment out of politics. It is by no means certain, however, that the seeds of future disagreement are removed. The current disputes as to the efficiency of the executive arrangement show that the west coast is in earnest and even yet is not fully satisfied that all which should be done has been accomplished. The whole subject of Japanese immigration is one which calls for careful settlement by a treaty which shall at the same time avoid antagonizing a proud nation and remove an element which unregulated can hardly avoid causing increasing uneasiness and ill feeling on the west coast.

*American Journal International Law, I, p. 450.

HOW CAN WE ENFORCE OUR EXCLUSION LAWS?

By Marcus Braun,

Immigrant Inspector, Department of Commerce and Labor, Washington, D. C.

From the Atlantic to the Pacific Ocean we have, I believe, on the Canadian border, a stretch of about 4,000 miles; the southern boundary from Brownsville to Tia Juana is, I believe, about 2,500 miles long, making a total of about 6,500 miles. On these two borders the United States Government maintains an immigrant inspection service consisting of perhaps all told 300 officers and other employees. These officers and employees, generally speaking, are a fine body of men, well trained and usually very much devoted to the service. At their disposal are the various laws and regulations which read very smoothly and which in theory are excellent. When it comes to practical enforcement, it is a different thing.

The best guarded border line that I know of in any country is in Russia, where the government places at every *wierst* (about nine-tenths of an English mile) an armed guard, day and night in three shifts for every twenty-four hours. These Russian frontier guards have the most far-reaching power and authority, they can arrest anybody who crosses the frontier, whether in possession of papers or not; they have a right to shoot, to kill, and yet, with this immense apparatus at their disposal, there are thousands and thousands of people smuggled out of Russia and smuggled into Russia. How much easier must be the smuggling of aliens across our northern and southern boundary lines. I am not in possession of the latest statistical data as to how many Japanese and Chinese officially entered within the last year into the United States, but I am sure that no matter how large or small the number is, many more entered the country surreptitiously.

The smuggling of Chinamen and Japanese is a regular profession on these two border lines; it is not a very risky undertaking, and it pays very well, from $25.00 to $200.00 per head. When I say that it is not a risky undertaking, I mean to indicate thereby that the smuggler of Chinamen and Japanese on the two borders very seldom crosses the border line; he merely brings his wards to the border and he tells them to run across. True, there may be on the American side someone or several persons who will show the way to these smuggled Chinamen and Japanese further, but if those men are caught, we can hardly get them convicted of having smuggled these Orientals into the country, because they merely picked them up on American soil and showed them the way.

Another bad feature is that the highly technical rules governing the admission of evidence before our tribunals make it many times almost impossible to secure convictions, aye, far worse, many Chinamen who were smuggled into the country during the night at some convenient place, have had and have the audacity to present themselves the next morning at the office of our Chinese inspector in charge, with an affidavit, made by someone in some interior city of the United States, in which affidavit it usually is stated that so and so is a merchant or a laundryman, residing for the last ten or fifteen years, to the knowledge of the affiant, in that particular city, and that so and so went on a pleasure trip or on a business trip to some particular place on or near the border line. Armed with such an affidavit, the Chinaman asks our Chinese inspector in charge to endorse his paper, in order that he may not be held up at the railroad station when trying to board a train to some interior point.

Experience has shown that when the inspector in charge refuses to make an endorsement on such a manufactured document, and places the Chinaman under arrest, he is subsequently admitted by the courts and commissioners, and thus becomes the possessor of a regular court document which is incontestable, and which is considered by the smuggling craft a far better and safer document than a *bona fide* Chinese certificate of residence.

As far as the Japanese are concerned, we are still worse off; there is no such thing as a Japanese exclusion law; by a proclamation of the President of the United States, the entry of Japanese laborers from Mexico and Canada is now prohibited if these Japanese are not in possession of passports from their government entitling them to go to the United States. When I made an investigation on the Mexican border concerning the enforcement of this order there, I found that the Japanese simply threw away their passports and crossed the border line at some convenient point; and once they were in the country it was next to impossible to get them out again, unless we could have them positively identified as having entered surreptitiously.

The topographical conditions on these two border lines make it easy for Japanese to smuggle themselves into the country or to be smuggled in, and the absence of any registration laws such as obtain in every European country with the exception of England, and obtain particularly in Asiatic countries, is a great assistance to smuggled aliens. If we really want to keep out Chinese, Japanese, and in fact other undesirable aliens, we will have to change our laws. In the first place, we need an alien registration law, that is to say, every alien should be required to bring with him a passport from his own government, possibly with a photograph to avoid the subsequent selling or exchanging the same, it should be required that the aliens keep on their person their passport which should be stamped at the time of their arrival, and that until they become citizens of the United States, they should be required to register their residence either with the local police or with a special bureau to be created for that purpose. They should also be held to notify promptly these authorities of any change of residence, and the penalty for failure to do so should be made very severe. Americans going abroad to take up their residence in foreign countries are compelled to do the same thing, and I do not see why we could not require aliens who come to the United States for continued or temporary sojourn to do likewise. The enactment of such a law would not only keep out inadmissible Orientals, but would keep out other undesirable aliens also.

As I stated before, our immigration service is composed of excellent men, our central organization at Washington is most perfect, but our laws are inadequate, and as far as the Chinese situation is concerned, positively bad. The Chinese exclusion law ought to be taken out of the hands of the United States commissioners and United States courts. The Secretary of the Department of Commerce and Labor ought to be the sole judge of whether a Chinaman has a right to be in the United States or not, the same as he is the sole judge of the right of any other alien to be in this country.

ENFORCEMENT OF THE CHINESE EXCLUSION LAW

By JAMES BRONSON REYNOLDS,
New York.

On the twenty-ninth day of the eleventh moon of Peng Ng year, that is, January 13, 1907, there appeared on the walls of many buildings in the Chinese quarter of Singapore a declaration from which I take the following statement: "In America we are one and all ill-treated as if we were criminals, no distinction being made between officials, merchants, students and ordinary people. There the disgrace inflicted upon us may be said to be carried to its fullest limit. . . . Given by Lam Hong Wai, the man who proposes to revive the boycott." The signer of this declaration was a well-known, prosperous Chinese merchant of Singapore, and his judgment on the American Bureau of Immigration, I am informed, voiced the general sentiment of intelligent Chinamen.

A few months previous to the above pronunciamento, I was visited by a Chinese merchant, who told me the following experience of a brother merchant of New York. A son of the latter, born in this country, hence entitled under the law to live here, had gone to Canton to receive a Chinese education. On the completion of his studies he returned to this country. Upon reaching San Francisco, in spite of the fact that he was a first-class passenger and carried papers establishing his American birth, he was stopped and confined in the "pen," the rough quarters in which detained immigrants were lodged. Upon his detention he wired his father, who at once started for San Francisco. The father found on arrival that his son had been ordered deported. The father retained an American lawyer, who appealed from the local decision on the case to the higher immigration authorities in Washington. Two days later the father was visited by a Chinese interpreter in the service of the American government, who told him that he had wasted time in appealing to Washington and that fifty dollars given to the right man would have "fixed" the case. The interpreter stated subsequently that even then one hundred dollars would arrange the matter. This amount was promptly paid and the next day the father and son started east.

Similar incidents were told me by Chinese merchants and officials as well as by American missionaries. Some of their tales were well substantiated; some were of doubtful truth. But unfortunately the fiction was not more discreditable than the truth. An able Chinese governor, since made viceroy, stated to me that though he desired to send students from his province to America, he was deterred from doing so by the treatment accorded to Chinese students at American ports of entry.

In his annual message to Congress in 1905, President Roosevelt said:

> In the effort to carry out the policy of excluding Chinese laborers— Chinese coolies—grave injustice and wrong have been done by this nation to the people of China, and, therefore, ultimately to this nation itself. Chinese students, business and professional men of all kinds—not only merchants, but bankers, doctors, manufacturers, professors, travelers and the like— should be encouraged to come here and treated on precisely the same footing that we treat students, business men, travelers and the like of other nations. . . . There would not be the least danger that any such provision would result in any relaxation of the law about laborers. These will under all conditions be kept out absolutely. But it will be more easy to see that both justice and courtesy are shown, as they ought to be shown, to other Chinese, if the law or treaty is framed as above suggested. Examinations should be completed at the port of departure from China.

In this message the President recommended that the laws be so altered as to permit the exempt classes, that is, those not laborers, to come and go freely, with the privileges granted to the same classes of other nationalities.

In his annual report to the President in 1907, Hon. Oscar S. Straus, Secretary of Commerce and Labor, said:

> The real purpose of the government's policy is to exclude a particular and well-defined class, leaving other classes of Chinese, except as they, together with all other foreigners, may be included within the prohibitions of the general immigration laws, as free to come and go as the citizens or subjects of any other nation. As the laws are framed, however, it would appear that the purpose was rigidly to exclude persons of the Chinese race in general and to admit only such persons of the race as fall within certain expressly stated exemptions—as if, in other words, exclusion was the rule

and admission the exception. I regard this feature of the present laws as unnecessary and fraught with irritating consequences.

The editor of a well-known Chinese paper in San Francisco, in a pamphlet on the treatment of the exempt classes of Chinese in the United States, states: "Chinese laborers of all classes have been excluded from the United States by mutual agreement, and the Chinese themselves are not now asking for any change in this arrangement, but they do ask for as fair treatment as other nationalities receive in relation to the exempt classes." He adds: "It is well known that the discourteous treatment of merchants and students by immigration officials was the principal cause of the boycott of American products in China in 1905."

In closing, the same writer quotes from an address delivered by Hon. William H. Taft when Secretary of War:

> Is it just that for the purpose of excluding or preventing perhaps one hundred Chinese coolies from slipping into this country against the law, we should subject an equal number of Chinese merchants and students of high character to an examination of such an inquisitorial, humiliating, insulting and physically uncomfortable character as to discourage altogether the coming of merchants and students? . . .
>
> Is it not the duty of members of Congress and of the Executive to disregard the unreasonable demand of a portion of the community, deeply prejudiced upon this subject in the Far West, and insist on extending justice and courtesy to a people from whom we are deriving and are likely to derive such immense benefit in the way of international trade?

In view of these statements from the highest American official authorities and from eminent Chinese in America and China, it should not surprise us that both the Chinese government and the Chinese people feel outraged and forcibly manifest their indignation and resentment. A tangible expression of this feeling in China was the boycott of American goods in 1905, which was not, I believe, a protest against the exclusion of Chinese laborers, but against the ill treatment of the exempt classes by our officials.

The statement of the Chinese editor previously quoted regarding the boycott is particularly significant in this connection. I had occasion to investigate the whole matter with much care. Statements made to me by the Chinese consul of San Francisco, a Yale graduate, by another university graduate, one of the secretaries of a recent imperial Chinese commission, by a Chinese Yale student highly commended by both faculty and students as to character and ability, by a former president of the Chinese Merchants' Association, and by Chinese merchants of Boston, New York and Buffalo, were all to the same effect. All admitted that Chinese merchants in America had substantially contributed to the boycott of American goods in China. My informants, however, unanimously denied that resentment aroused by our exclusion of Chinese laborers was the inciting cause.[1] But they asserted that the brutal treatment of merchants and students, belonging to the exempt classes, when seeking admission to this country, the blackmail merchants had been forced by subordinate government officials to pay for privileges to which they were legally entitled and the lack of security of person and property which they had experienced led them to aid the boycott. They alleged, however, that they were as anxious as our government to prevent the smuggling of laborers into this country and assigned three reasons therefor: first, such smuggling of ignorant laborers gave the Chinese merchants a bad name and hence injured their business; second, the smuggled coolies came to them in distress and were a financial burden upon them; third, these smuggled coolies often became low grade merchants and managers of disreputable dens, thus further discrediting the merchant class.

The Chinese merchants also bitterly complained of the selection of interpreters made by our government. The merchants held that these interpreters were not in any sense representative of the better elements of the Chinese communities. So strongly did the Chinese Merchants' Association of New York distrust the interpreter assigned to that port, that in 1903 it endorsed its president, a Chinese merchant of independent means, for the position of official interpreter. This position he agreed to accept in order to serve the Chinese community, though the salary was undoubtedly much smaller than the profits of his business.

Referring again to the boycott, it is but fair to state that our immigration officials in contradiction to the authorities above quoted, have insisted that the boycott was due to the desire of various classes in China and in this country to have the exclusion law so modified

---

[1] It was doubtless true that *in China* American exclusion of Chinese laborers was denounced and that both Chinese merchants and students in their public speeches there condemned our government for its action.

that coolies could more easily be admitted. The Bureau of Immigration calls attention to the fact that in the years 1903 to 1905, inclusive, 1,245 certificates were issued in China to those declaring themselves to be merchants, but that 22 per cent of these applicants were obviously not members of the exempt classes but laborers not entitled to enter the country, and consequently were rejected. Regarding these statistics a report of the bureau states: "It is confidently believed that many, perhaps a majority of the remaining 968, were also laborers, but had been so carefully coached and prepared beforehand that it was not possible to 'controvert' the prima facie evidence of their certificates and whose admission, therefore, was unavoidable." The bureau also calls attention to the fact that out of 2,218 Chinese who applied for admission to this country during the years 1904 and 1905, 642, or about 35 per cent, were rejected. The bureau believes the business of smuggling Chinese coolies to be so profitable that a large proportion of the Chinese merchants in this country have been directly or indirectly interested in it. A pamphlet issued by the bureau containing an elaborate defense of its action in a number of cases where its officials had been criticized, seeks to establish that the officials have merely enforced the exact provisions of the law and that difficulties have resulted only where individuals have failed to supply themselves with the admission papers required by our laws. But these views of the Bureau of Immigration do not seem to me sound, and its statements in regard to our Chinese communities unduly emphasize the dark side.

If the free admission of Chinese coolies were the price of a better understanding with China, it could not be paid. With but few exceptions it may be accepted as the universal judgment of our country that the admission of Chinese laborers with their low standard of living would injure the just interests of American labor, embitter our politics by another race issue, establish congested Chinese communities difficult to regulate, and be in many other ways an injury to our country and an embarrassment to local and national administrations. Chinese laborers must, therefore, be excluded.

The successful and tactful exclusion of the resourceful coolies is, it must be admitted, a very difficult task. It is my purpose to indicate the main difficulties in the way of the enforcement of the exclusion law and to point out that the task could be made easier and the immigration service more efficient through a more intelligent understanding of the whole situation and through the exercise of proper discrimination in the enforcement of the law.

It is of course impossible to state how many Chinese enter our country each year illegally. From reliable information which I received in 1907, I estimated that during that year from 2,000 to 5,000 crossed our borders. In an official report of facts concerning the enforcement of the Chinese exclusion laws published by the Bureau of Immigration in 1906, it was stated that the "bureau does not hesitate to express the opinion that many Chinamen, perhaps hundreds, cross the Mexican boundary into the United States every year." The inspector in charge at El Paso stated in his annual report dated June 30, 1905, that "during the past fiscal year 486 coolies are known to have arrived in Juarez, probably forty-six coolies found employment in Juarez, practically one hundred left for other border points, so that approximately 320 coolies have disappeared near the international boundary line in the vicinity of El Paso, and doubtless gained unlawful entry." He adds that it is believed that "the handling (*i. e.*, smuggling) of Chinese coolies is the sole occupation of perhaps one-third of the Chinese population of El Paso." It may be explained that El Paso is directly across the Rio Grande from the Mexican city of Juarez and favorably located for smuggling.

Smuggling on the Mexican border and on the northwestern Canadian border is well known, but few probably realize that smuggling of coolies goes on steadily across the northeastern Canadian border and into the cities of New York and Boston. In 1906 I learned that during the months of July, August and September about seventy-five coolies were smuggled into the port of Boston. During the spring of 1907 I was informed by Chinese merchants in Buffalo that from two to four coolies were being smuggled into that port weekly.

The smuggling business is very profitable. From $200 to $300 is said to be charged for bringing in a coolie, the latter being compelled to pay off his debt from his first earnings after his entrance into the country. Dr. J. Endicott Gardiner, an inspector and chief interpreter at San Francisco, estimated the cost of bringing a coolie from China and landing him in New York State to be

$300. The items reported are significant: $20 for the perjured testimony, $20 as commission to the middleman for obtaining the applicant, $20 toward what is called 'the government interpreter's fund,' $80 for the attorney, and the balance for transportation, incidental expenses, and the members of the ring." These figures agree with my own inquiries and are probably a fair average of the amount expended and the method of its distribution.

Several difficulties in the enforcement of the law must be admitted. First: Long stretches of territory covering thousands of miles must be protected by a few moderately paid officials, many of whom occupy uncomfortable quarters on the border most unwillingly. While on the whole, most of them probably render honest service during regular working hours, it is not surprisng that they are indisposed to turn night into day in order to catch a few alert Chinamen whose resources or those of their friends seem to be unlimited, since they always have friends on the American side ready to help them and can always secure the help of able American counsel in case our officials are guilty of any technical error in procedure.

Second: Because of the high prices paid for smuggling Chinamen, the smuggling system has been well organized. The band of smugglers at any given point usually consists of one or two American citizens, a couple of Chinamen, with sometimes a Chinese interpreter or an immigrant inspector as side partners. The service rendered by the dishonest inspector is usually to "tip off" the doings of the other officials. He may also give notice that on a certain night the inspectors may not be on duty or will be watching at a particular point, leaving other points uncovered. Allied with the smugglers and dishonest officials are the train hands on freight trains crossing the Mexican and Canadian borders. A brakeman can always secure $15 apiece for every Chinaman allowed to crawl into an empty freight car or otherwise conceal himself on the train with the brakeman's assistance or connivance. A conductor may get more. Undoubtedly some trainmen refuse to engage in this traffic, but many yield to the temptation to make a few dollars "on the side." The sentiment of the majority seems not to condemn the practice of smuggling Chinamen, especially as the help required from the trainmen is usually negative. It was recently stated by a high official of one of the railway unions that such smuggling could be stopped if the trainmen's unions would take aggressive action to suppress it.

In view, therefore, of the extent of territory to be protected, the money available for bribery and the number of American and Chinese smugglers, it must be admitted that the enforcement of the exclusion law is difficult. But an examination of the facts leads one to the conclusion that certain important improvements in the service could and should be instituted.

First: The Chinese interpreters should be of a better grade. Our immigrant officials are largely in the hands of Chinese inter-preters. This is inevitable, as few Americans speak Chinese. The dialects spoken by the Chinese coolies are unknown to Americans, except missionaries. The statements of the Chinese interpreters as a rule are, therefore, final and authoritative. Two or three inter-preters whom I know are men of excellent character and have ren-dered faithful and loyal service, meriting high praise as well as more substantial compensation than they have received. Careful inquiry regarding the majority, however, shows that their origin and education do not sufficiently qualify them for the task. Ordinary laundrymen and low grade Chinese waiters have often been made interpreters. Such interpreters, if honest, are not likely to be equal to the task given them and their associates are probably in the coolie class of each community. Many of their most inti-mate friends and daily associates have entered the country in viola-tion of the law. Why should they not favor their friends if they can do so when the chances of their being caught are very slight? With every appearance of honesty, strengthened by ostentatious roughness toward their countrymen in the presence of inspectors, they can entirely thwart the efforts of inspectors by tipping off in-tended raids, by informing their smuggler friends of the intended action of the inspectors, or by misinterpreting or mistranslating. The weak point, which is also the essential point, of our whole exclu-sion work rests with the Chinese interpreters, and if exclusion is to be effective, this service must be entrusted to intelligent men whose habits and associations are well known. These interpreters should be drawn not from the coolie class, as has been too largely the case in the past, but from the merchant class, since the latter class, as I have indicated, favors the enforcement of the exclusion law. It would be wise to establish these men in grades so that faithful and efficient service would be rewarded by promotion and increased pay.

Upon a suggestion that I made two or three years ago a chief interpreter was appointed to have supervision over the entire force of interpreters. The first selection was, however, unfortunate, and after some delay the incumbent was removed. Such a supervisory official, however, is highly important to both the honesty and efficiency of the service.

The second important improvement should be a more careful distinction between the different classes of Chinamen. With some exceptions the immigration officials have failed utterly to establish friendly relations with those Chinamen who are in sympathy with the exclusion law, thereby to secure their coöperation in its enforcement. As previously indicated, the writer learned that a large body of Chinese merchants in this country is unfavorable to the importation of coolies and anxious to see the exclusion law strictly enforced.

How valuable their help might be is illustrated by a personal experience. In the summer of 1906, upon the request and authorization of President Roosevelt, I investigated the smuggling of coolies. Having established friendly relations with Chinese merchants in several eastern cities, I asked proof of their assertion that they knew that smuggling of coolies was then going on and that they were willing to join in its suppression. They agreed to make good both on their charge of smuggling and on their ability and willingness to help in its detection. The city of Boston was selected to test their declarations. The Chinese merchants of that city declared that in July and August of that year two parties of coolies, numbering about fifty, had been smuggled into that city by sailboat from Newfoundland under the very noses of the immigration officials. They stated that a third party would arrive in September and that I should be fully informed so that I could witness its landing. In due time I was told that the party had left St. Johns in a chartered yacht and would land on the New England coast at a certain date. Shortly before its arrival a notice in Chinese appeared on the walls of Chinatown in Boston warning the friends of the incoming coolies that the government had learned of their approach. The government's information came about in this way: It chanced that one of the smugglers upon the receipt of his pay for the August expedition got drunk and openly boasted of his smuggling achievement.

Through his statements suspicions were excited which resulted in the discovery of the projected September expedition. An inspector was sent to Halifax to head off the coolies at that point, but the fact that the inspector had been sent and the assumed name under which he traveled were given out by the chief Chinese inspector to the Boston press before the inspector reached Halifax. This useful information was probably telegraphed at once to the Chinese in Halifax.

On the morning of the landing of the coolies a Boston paper stated that a United States revenue cutter had been sent at full speed to Portland, Maine, as the government had been led to believe that the coolies were to be landed at that point. On the same day, upon information furnished by my friends, the Chinese merchants, I proceeded to Providence, where I witnessed the actual landing of the party at two o'clock in the morning. A description of the assistant smuggler who would receive the party, the time of his arrival in Providence from Boston, and the house to which he would go and to which the coolies would be taken were told me in advance. I personally verified all these particulars. This information was given to me because a former Chinese inspector who had the wisdom to establish friendly relations with the Chinese merchants and had treated them courteously put me in touch with them and backed my request for assistance.

This party of coolies would probably have been successfully entered without the Bureau of Immigration being any the wiser, but that, after the first two lots had been landed and housed, the smugglers felt so secure that they landed the rest of the coolies in a group. Several of these were found hiding in the grass by some workmen, who telephoned to the police and this remnant of the party was arrested.

I am quite aware that it is generally believed that the Chinese communities in our cities are composed of gamblers, opium eaters, smugglers and other law breakers. Doubtless these communities have their fair proportion of disorderly characters, but they do not monopolize gambling games in our cities, and though some of them take opium instead of alcohol, the difference is one of taste rather than character. There are, however, in our eastern cities, at least in each Chinese community, a considerable number of reputable, intelligent merchants devoting themselves strictly to business, living orderly lives and desiring to be law-abiding and law-promoting citizens. These men who may not be known to the police or to our slumming parties, might be sought out by our officials, and as I have shown from my own experience, they could render invaluable service in making our exclusion laws effective.

A short time before the smuggling expedition just described, I had an interview with five Chinese merchants in Boston. One of them had a son at Harvard, and another a son at Yale. They talked as soberly and fairly as successful American merchants would have talked and explained fully to me the difficulties under whi-'- they were living in our country and the indignities to which they had been subjected by American immigration officials. It was only after they were convinced of my own good will and my authori y to speak for the President that I secured their coöperation. Once pledged, however, their word was loy '!y kept; they never failed me at any point and made good though much trouble and effort were required to do so.

The third important improvement should be in the better organizatio of the Bureau of Immigration. The present organization of the bureau seems to me to be inadequate for its important tasks. It has two functions of a fundamentally different nature; the reception and handling of immigrants entering the Atlantic ports, of whom 98 per cent are admitted after careful sifting, and the reception and exclusion of Oriental immigrants on the Pacific coast which is quite the reverse of that on the Atlantic coas The sta...ons on the Pacific coast are far apart, some of them remote and uncomfortable. They need frequent visiting by proper officials constantly in touch and in correspondence with the heads of these offices. The Chinese or Oriental bureau should, therefore, in my opinion, be organized independently with its own chief and a deputy chief or general supervisor.

A fourth needed improvement of the highest importance is the thorough examination by the American consuls in China of Chinese applying for admission to this country. As President Roosevelt stated the case in his annual message to Congress in 1905: "Examinations should be completed at the port of departure." Additions to the office force of various consuls were recommended by President Roosevelt so that this added work might be promptly and thoroughly performed. The task of the immigration officials at the ports of entry would then be merely to satisfy themselves that those producing the consular certificates were the parties to whom they had been issued.

The late Commissioner General Sargent recommended, I believe, that special commissioners of immigration should be placed at Hongkong and Shanghai, who should investigate and issue certificates. This would place the entire matter under the Bureau of Immigration and would eliminate misunderstanding or friction between government departments. Either of these remedies would contribute to the more successful exclusion of coolies and the elimination of delays and discourtesies in dealing with the exempt classes. The enforcement of the exclusion law at best is attendant with many difficulties. Its defective or brutal enforcement may embarrass our relations with China and seriously injure our commercial and diplomatic relations with the entire East. These relations are recognized to be of growing importance demanding the most serious attention.

Our own ignorance of Chinese conditions and classes both in China and in this country and our ignorance of the Chinese language which compels us to accept implicitly the statements of Chinese interpreters, are serious handicaps in our dealing with the Chinese. Our past failure to secure interpreters of proper grade, our consequent inability properly to handle the exempt classes, and the untrustworthiness of the certificates supplied by our own consuls have further augmented our difficulties. At present our consular service is undoubtedly far more trustworthy than formerly. Its investigations could prevent the abuse of consular certificates and could remove the delays and indignities endured by members of the exempt classes at our ports. Improvement in the grade and intelligence of interpreters, proper promotion for efficient service, establishment of the Chinese bureau as an independent branch of the immigration service under able management, the relentless pursuit of smugglers, both American and Chinese, and a better understanding of the Chinese communities in this country would make our exclusion policy more successful and promote good will in our political and commercial relations with the Orient.

PART FOUR

The Problem of Oriental Immigration Outside of America

SOURCES AND CAUSES OF JAPANESE EMIGRATION
BY YOSABURO YOSHIDA,
UNIVERSITY OF WISCONSIN, MADISON, WIS.

ORIENTAL IMMIGRATION INTO THE PHILIPPINES
BY RUSSELL McCULLOCH STORY, A.M.,
HARVARD UNIVERSITY, CAMBRIDGE, MASS.

ORIENTAL LABOR IN SOUTH AFRICA
BY L. E. NEAME,
JOHANNESBURG, SOUTH AFRICA; AUTHOR OF "THE ASIATIC DANGER IN THE COLONIES"

JAPANESE IMMIGRATION INTO KOREA
BY THOMAS F. MILLARD,
NEW YORK CITY; AUTHOR OF "THE NEW FAR EAST" AND "AMERICA AND THE FAR EASTERN QUESTION"

THE EXCLUSION OF ASIATIC IMMIGRANTS IN AUSTRALIA
BY PHILIP S. ELDERSHAW, B.A., and P. P. OLDEN,
UNIVERSITY LAW SCHOOL, SYDNEY, NEW SOUTH WALES

SOURCES AND CAUSES OF JAPANESE EMIGRATION

By Yosaburo Yoshida,
University of Wisconsin, Madison, Wis.

"Home, home, sweet home, there's no place like home." Yet, leaving the fatherland of mountains and waters, many a Japanese seeks a new life in a strange land across the Pacific. There must be strong causes for this movement.

The question arises whether there is any political pressure upon the emigrant. Japan is one of the most progressive nations in the world, and there exists no discontent with the present rule of the constitutional government. Is there any religious cause bringing him here? Article eighteen of the imperial constitution guarantees freedom of religious belief. No persecution for difference of religion exists, as neither Buddhist nor Christian is treated as heathen in Japan. Is there any race prejudice or animosity? The whole Japanese population is of one race, consequently there is no oppressed race nor one dominant over another. Does the strict operation of the law enforcing military duty drive a portion of her youths here? No people are more patriotic than this race of little brown men. The fifty millions of Japanese souls will gladly throw their bodies into fire at command of their Great Sire.

Then, what are the causes of Japanese emigration? I recognize and shall discuss three: increase of population, economic pressure, and inducement, or attraction.

Increase of Population

Increase of population is closely connected with economic pressure upon the laboring classes. But I shall describe here chiefly the former, and will discuss the latter afterwards.

No statistics of Japanese population are reliable until 1872. The increasing rate since that year has been as follows:[1]

Year.	Per Cent.	Year.	Per Cent
1872	.57	1890	.95
1873	.98	1891	.66
1874	1.11	1892	.91
1875	1.00	1893	.73
1876	...	1894	1.03
1877	...	1895	1.09
1878	...	1896	1.04
1879	.45	1897	1.22
1880	1.20	1898	1.24
1881	.94	1899	1.14
1882	.86	1900	1.25
1883	1.17	1901	1.39
1884	1.11	1902	1.29
1885	.84	1903	1.54
1886	.84	1904	1.14
1887	1.46	1905	1.13
1888	1.38	1906	1.14
1889	1.17	1907	1.15

The above figures show that population is increasing year after year, and if the increase continues at the present rate the population will be doubled after sixty years.

Population increases, but the area of the land is limited, consequently the density of population per square ri[2] has been increasing at the following rates: 1872, 1,335; 1882, 1,385; 1892, 1,657; 1903, 1,885.

According to the general statistics, Japan in density of population ranks below only Belgium, Holland and England. These three nations get their food materials by importation from other countries; Japan is feeding herself.

I have described the rapid growth of population in Japan as a whole, but, if we ask ourselves whether those districts where population is most dense are the districts which contribute the largest number of emigrants, our answer is negative. The districts of Hiroshima, Yamaguchi, Wakayama and Fukuoka are not very dense in population, and their birth rates are also less than the average rate for the whole of Japan.[3] Yet these districts always contribute the

[1] "The Financial and Economic Annual of Japan," 1905, p. 3; 1907, p. 2.
[2] Square ri equals 5.9552 square miles.
[3] "Movement de la population de L'empire du Japon," 1905, Proportion, P. 1.

dominant number to Japanese emigration. The districts of Kinai, where the successive emperors fixed their capital for more than twenty-five centuries, and where consequently the population is the most dense in the country, are not sections which drive emigrants abroad. Because of these facts, some writers urge that there is no direct connection between increasing population and Japanese emigration.[4]

But I consider the density of population a cause of emigration if we take the country as a whole. It is not the cause if we take district by district. The reason is very evident. Although some districts are very densely populated, if their economic capacity is sufficient to maintain their population, then it is not necessary to migrate. Furthermore, the peculiar character and environment of the people differ by districts. For example, the region of Kinai, with charming scenery, although crowded with a toiling population, renders the nature of the people very strong in home affection. Moreover, the family system is very ancient, and the people are amiable and submissive. On the contrary, the people of the regions from Hiroshima extending towards the southwestern districts, are venturesome and enterprising. The districts in Kinai have been the home of poets, artists and men of letters, while the southwestern part has supported pirates and warriors. That the increasing population is a profound cause for emigration can be seen more clearly if we consider it in connection with the economic pressure upon Japan's lower classes.

Economic Pressure

In this world-stage of the twentieth century, where many nations are competing with each other to become the dominant power, the rapid growth of population is a rather happy and desirable thing for our island empire, situated on the Eastern Sea. But this great movement, necessary from the viewpoint of further expansion of the empire, has a bad effect upon the classes who are toiling at the bottom of the present community. "The more poor the more babies," the Japanese proverb frankly runs. It is from these lower class people that the largest number of children come, and consequently the increase of population brings more laborers. The competition among the working classes in a country where the

4 T. Okawahira, "The Nippon Imin-ron." Tokyo, 1905, pp. 36-37.

area of land is limited, where no national labor organization exists, where no labor legislation operates, results in vast millions of struggling creatures spending their daily lives under the economic pressure of landlords and capitalists in a hopeless and stricken condition.

The area of the cultivated land was only 5,193,762 cho in 1904,[5] that is, 17 per cent of the whole area. The average holding of land owned by one farmer is only 9 tan 8 se.[6] The annual yield from such a small piece of land, less than three acres, even under the most perfect system of utilization, is absolutely insufficient to support a family according to modern standards of comfort. Under such an economic condition the peasant class, which constitutes the bulk of the Japanese emigration to the United States, are spending their days. The fact that the districts which contribute the largest number of emigrants contain always the greatest percentage of the peasant class is shown below.

Geographical Sources of Emigrants

Basing our figures upon the number of passports issued by each district during the five years from 1899 to 1903, the number of emigrants to foreign countries, excluding Korea and China, is as follows:[7]

TABLE I.

District.	No. of passports issued.	District.	No. of passports issued.
Hiroshima	21,871	Fukushima	1,613
Kumamoto	12,149	Yehime	948
Yamaguchi	11,219	Aichi	767
Fukuoka	7,698	Fukui	683
Niigata	6,698	Shiga	646
Wakayama	3,750	Saga	624
Nagasaki	3,548	Twenty-seven other districts.	5,041
Hyogo	3,532		
Okayama	2,176	Total	84,576
Miyagi	1,613		

[5] M. Togo, "The Nippon Shokumin-ron," Tokyo, 1906, p. 180. A cho equals 2.4507 acres.

[6] Tan equals 0.2451 acre, Se equals 119 square yards.

[7] M. Togo, "The Nippon Shokumin-ron," pp. 269-271; also Okawahira, "The Nippon Imin-ron," pp. 38-40.

Number of passports issued for emigrants, 1899-1903. Each circle represents 500 emigrants. There is no emigration from the northern island which is not represented here.

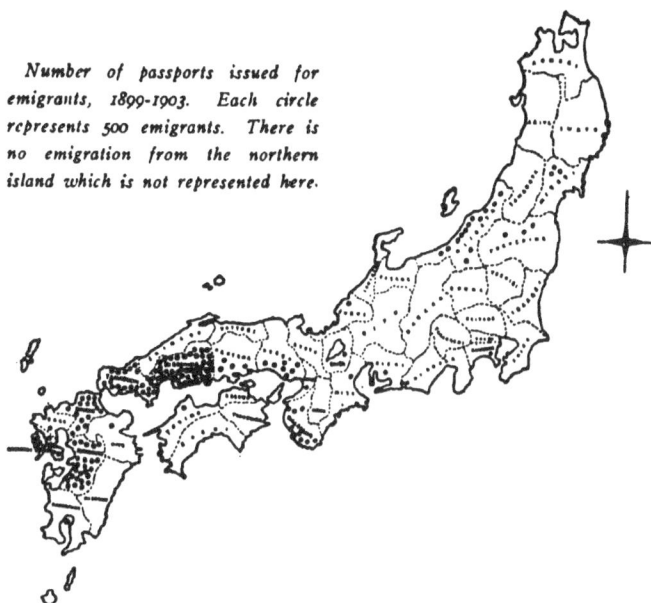

Although the above statistics include emigrants to all foreign countries excepting China and Korea, more than 80 per cent of the total number came to the United States. The area of farm land cultivated by the Japanese in the State of California in 1908, classified by their native districts, was as follows:

TABLE II.[a]

Cultivated by immigrants from the district of—	Area of farm land in California—acres.
Hiroshima	33,443
Wakayama	30,905
Fukuoka	14,833
Kumamoto	14,827
Yamaguchi	10,598
Aichi	10,268
Okayama	6,334
Other districts	33,594½
Total	154,802½

[a] "The Japanese-American Year Book," 1909, the first appendix, pp. 3-4.

The table indicates that the immigrants from the district of Hiroshima[9] cultivate the largest area of farm land. Next comes the district of Wakayama. Each district controls about one-fifth of all the farm land cultivated by the Japanese in California. In 1905 nearly 50,000 of the 74,000 total Japanese population in Hawaii were from the three districts of Hiroshima, Kumamoto and Yamaguchi.[10]

I have already mentioned the geographical section of Japan from which most of her emigrants come. Then, what is the peculiar character of those people? What are the economic conditions in those districts? Generally speaking, the people of the Sanyodo, where the districts of Hiroshima, Yamaguchi and Okayama are situated, were warriors in the feudal ages; and, the districts being along the coast, the people were accustomed to go to sea, and were venturesome and eager to satisfy new wants. The fundamental cause of emigration is the economic condition of the districts. The percentage of small farmers in those districts is as follows:

TABLE III.[11]

Districts.	Percentage of agricultural families which cultivate less than 8 tan.
Hiroshima	70
Wakayama	Unknown
Fukuoka	56
Kumamoto	Unknown
Yamaguchi	61
Aichi	Unknown
Okayama	66
Hyogo	73
Yehime	68

The number of small farmers is more than 50 per cent in all the above districts. Hyogo is the district which is populated with

[9] "Most emigrants in the district of Hiroshima come from the counties of Aki, Saeki, Takada, and cities of Hiroshima and Toyoda. When they start as emigrants, their land and houses are in the hands of landlords; their position is that of small tenant. But when they come back after four or five years' labor abroad, they usually buy a house and two or three tans of farm land, and become independent farmers, or merchants. . . . About six-tenths of all emigrants succeed in this way," etc.—"The Osaka Mainichi Shimbun," November 9, 1904, quoted by Okawahira.

[10] T. Okawahira, "The Nippon Imin-ron," p. 89.

[11] These statistics are based upon an investigation made by the Department of Agriculture and Commerce of Japan in 1888; it is presumed that there is not much change in the present condition.

the largest percentage of small farmers of all districts in Japan. The district of Hiroshima, the center of emigration, comes next with its 70 per cent of peasant families. If we investigate the average area of cultivated land per capita of the agricultural population in the respective districts, the effect upon emigration can be seen with more clearness.

TABLE IV.[12]

		Tan.
Hiroshima	....	.11
Wakayama	....	Unknown
Fukuoka	....	.19
Kumamoto	....	Unknown
Yamaguchi	....	.17
Aichi	....	Unknown
Okayama	....	.15
Hyogo	....	.14
Nagasaki	....	.15
Yehime	....	.18

The average amount of farm land per capita in Hiroshima is not only the smallest among the above-mentioned immigrant districts, but also among all districts in Japan. Yamaguchi, Ohayama and Hyogo are also below the average.

A remarkable fact is noticeable here, that the district of Hiroshima, where the average holding of farm land was smallest among all Japanese districts in 1888, contributed the largest number of Japanese who cultivate farm land in America in 1908.

More than this, the wealth per capita in those districts is below the average amount of wealth per capita in Japan. According to Messrs. Igarashi and Takahashi,[13] the average wealth per capita of Japan is 505.755 yen, while that of Hiroshima is 381.895, of Yamaguchi is 489.005, of Wakayama is 351.675, and so on.

Inducement and Attraction

No advertisement has ever appeared in the Japanese newspapers inducing emigrants to go to the United States. But the most effective advertisement is the stories of success of Japanese in America, which occasionally appear in the papers and magazines.

---

[12] M. Togo, "The Nippon Shokumin-ron," pp. 141-143.
[13] E. Igarashi and H. Takahashi, "The National Wealth of Japan," Table I.

Whenever certain Japanese return to Japan they talk with the newspaper reporter, telling how they struggled in a penniless condition, how they saved money, what industry they started, or how many acres of land they own in America. Such articles in a local newspaper, accompanied by illustrations, usually make a strong impression upon the young peasant or rough country lad. Thus, the account of success of Mr. Kinya Ushizima, the "potato king" in California, appeared many times before the public and, it seems, induced many emigrants to leave home, especially from the district of Fukuoka, from which Mr. Ushizima himself emigrated many years ago. The success of Mr. Domoto, as the greatest flower raiser west of the Rockies, attracted many young farmers from his native district of Wakayama.

There have been many pamphlets published, some printed in more than thirty editions, under such titles as "How to Succeed in America," "Guide Book to Different Occupations in America," "Guide Book to America," "The New Hawaii," etc. All these books are written by those who returned from America or are still resident in this country. Generally speaking, they have exaggerated the abundance of opportunities in the United States and have stimulated emigration in over-attractive descriptions. . Correspondence with Japanese laborers who are already in this country has also some influence.[14] But the sphere of this kind of inducement is very narrow, limited to the correspondent's relatives or friends at home. The inducements and attractions above mentioned are the result of the simple fact that labor earns more in America than in Japan.

The conclusion which can be drawn from the facts already mentioned in this paper is this, that a large proportion of the Japanese emigration comes from the peasant class in the districts of the south; and growing population, economic pressure and inducement or attraction combine to cause their emigration. No doubt there are countless minor causes operating on individuals, such as ill-luck in business, a bad crop of rice, sudden death of the devoted wife, frequent visits of the bill collectors, or simply desire to see great America. But the fundamental and principal causes are those already mentioned.

[14]"The Seventh Biennial Report of the Bureau of Labor Statistics of the State of California," 1896, p. 108.

Motives of Japanese Emigration by Classes

During the year 1906 the Japanese government issued 8,466 passports to the continental United States and 30,093 to Hawaii. The purposes for which the passports were granted were as follows:[15]

	Official Duties.	Study.	Commercial Business.	Agriculture and Fishing.	Artisan.	Labor.	Traveling.	Miscellaneous.
To the continental United States...	43	2,825	1,215	1,046	22	462	2	2,851
To Hawaii	7	17	132	28,756	7	1,051	0	423

Among the eight groups above quoted, I take for discussion only two which include the greater portion of emigrants: the farmers and the students.

Farmers: This class consists of those who are engaged in agricultural pursuits, either as tenants or as farm laborers. They belong to the lower classes of the Japanese community, if not to the lowest of all. They are the real corner-stone of the nation, but they are poor. In this class of emigrants the most conservative, uneducated and innocent persons can be found. The greater number of them being quite ignorant of foreign conditions, they are usually cared for and transported by the so-called "emigration companies."[16] Farm laborers whose daily wages are an average of only thirty-two sen[17] (sixteen cents), have hardly an opportunity to accumulate money enough to escape from their own group. The sole motive of this emigration is simply "to make money," and nothing more.

Generally speaking, when a European emigrant is bidding farewell to his home, his intention is, perhaps, to go to a new land where he can start a new life. His desire is to find a new society around him and to build up a new home. In short, he is going to be an

15 "The Twenty-sixth Annual Statistical Report of the Japanese Empire," p. 67.
16 There were thirty-six companies or individuals engaging in exporting Japanese laborers in 1903, with capital ranging from 1,000,000 yen to 20,000 yen.
17 "The Seventh Financial and Economic Annual of Japan," 1907, p. 75.

American himself. The contrary is true of the Japanese whose only desire is to build up a new home, not upon American soil, but in his native land. He desires to save a certain amount of money by a four or five-year struggle, and then, coming back to his own land, to start in business or become an independent farmer. He does not desire to exhibit the fruits of his toil before an American audience, but only before his fellow-countrymen.

Students: Since 1870 Japanese students have been coming to this country, and between 1885 and 1890, the period of political transformation to constitutional government, many students and politicians who failed to realize their ambitions came to this country. They worked as "school boys" or domestic servants and studied in leisure moments. The students in those days were able to get kind assistance from the Board of Foreign Missions in this country.[18] When they returned to Japan after several years' hard study, they were offered responsible positions in governmental service, as Japan was eager to adopt western institutions. Among those old "school boys" to-day many distinguished persons can be found: diplomatists, educators and writers.

At present many students are coming to this country, more than 90 per cent of them with scanty means, but with high ambitions, recalling the old days of their eminent forerunners. There were 951 students in a total of 2,261 Japanese immigrants admitted during the three months of April, May and June of 1907,[19] and of the total number, 9,544, admitted to continental America in 1908, 2,252 were students.[20] Estimating from the above statistics, the number of students who have come to this country since the early period runs into the thousands.

These students are graduates of Japanese high schools or certain professional institutions. They cross the ocean with abundance of hope, determined to dare what those famous Japanese used to dare years ago. Their ambition is to study, but most of them, perhaps 999 in 1,000, after undergoing bitter experiences in isolation, usually lose their ambition and take up other vocations. Thus a Japanese servant confesses before the American public, that "Some say the Japanese are studying while they are working in the kitchen, but it

[18] I. Nitobe, "The Intercourse between the United States and Japan," Baltimore, 1891, pp. 165-6.
[19] "Annual Report of the Commissioner-General of Immigration," 1907, p. 76.
[20] *Ibid.*, 1908, p. 90.

is all nonsense. Many of them started so, but nearly all of them failed."[21]

The difficulty of studying as self-supporting students changes those students to common domestic servants or farm laborers. Their intentions were laudable and their hopes were very high; but later these intentions and hopes, which they ever declared before parents and sweethearts, must be cast away after much discouragement. The man who fails of his expected goal in a strange land after a long struggle naturally becomes, in most cases, irresponsible. Among the gang of laborers which sail to Alaska every spring you may find many young Japanese who quitted their native land to study American civilization in college classes. They are "not only lazy and worthless, but are constantly raising a disturbance."[22]

The two classes mentioned here are not the lowest people of the low classes, nor the worst and most unfit people. There is a certain defective class of people, such as tramps, beggars, ex-convicts and paupers, in Japan as elsewhere. They have no ambition to elevate their own standard of living by any economic means. They are spending a dull, changeless life in an ever-changing community. If any person in this country believes that the Japanese government sends or encourages these undesirable people to emigrate to this country it is a great mistake. This class of people has no relation to the dynamic side of the Japanese community. Even in dreams they would not desire to migrate far away over the ocean to the land of opportunity. Opportunity is worthless to them, for they are satisfied in their own condition.

[21] "The Confession of a Japanese Servant," "Independent," Vol. 59, p. 667.
[22] "The Bulletin of the United States Fish Commission," Vol. XXI, 1901, p. 185.

ORIENTAL IMMIGRATION INTO THE PHILIPPINES

By Russell McCulloch Story, A.M.,
Harvard University, Cambridge, Mass.

The problems of immigration with which the United States has had to deal have not been confined, since 1899, to the Western Hemisphere alone. The importance of regulating immigration into the Philippines was early realized after their acquisition by this country. The questions to be met were in many ways more complex than those connected with immigration into the United States, owing, in part, to the proximity of the islands to the Asiatic mainland. The solutions possible were restricted within the limits determined by American law, peonage and serfdom in any form thus being impossible; and in addition the attitude of the Filipino peoples on the general question was, of necessity, a consideration of fundamental importance. Fortunately, in the latter case, there has been no great difference in sentiment between the governed race and its governors.

The majority of Oriental immigrants into the Philippines have been furnished by China and Japan. China alone contributes almost the entire body of immigrants that seek admission from Asiatic countries into the islands. Hence, as far as the Philippines are concerned, the question of Oriental immigration almost resolves itself into a discussion of the policy of Chinese exclusion which has been carried out by the United States' administration of the archipelago.[1] For this reason the chief attention in the following pages is given to the questions arising from the presence or exclusion of the Chinese immigrants.

No one can study the reports of the Schurman and subsequent Philippine commissions, or the Philippine census reports, and fail to be impressed with the wonderful resources of the Philippines. It was the expectation of the civilized world that following their acquisition by the United States a tremendous impetus would be

[1] Cf. "The Problem of the Chinese in the Philippines," in "The American Political Science Review," February, 1909.

given to the development of these resources. This expectation early gained ground in China, and the Chinese government was keenly alive to the opportunities which might thus be opened up to the activities of many of its citizens. Even before the action of the United States military in applying the exclusion laws of the United States to the Philippines, the State Department at Washington had been given to understand that China would protest against any such action.

The basis for exclusion in the Philippines must rest almost entirely on three propositions, viz., the right of the Filipino races to develop themselves and their own resources, racial and commercial, without the assistance or stimulating presence of the Chinese; a desire to prevent the growth of a racial question through the antagonism or unfortunate amalgamation of two different races such as the Malay and the Mongolian; and in the third place the desire of the United States to be able to sustain its own immigration and exclusion laws against possible migrations of Chinese from the Philippines to the States.

A study of the immigration statistics since 1898 shows that the greatest number of Chinese entering the islands was immediately following American occupation. This high tide continued until 1904, despite the exclusion restrictions, the excess of arrivals over departures up to 1904 being 8,562. In the same year the registration of the Chinese showed that there were approximately fifty thousand of them resident in the Philippines. This number has steadily increased since that time, though the gross number of Chinese immigrants has apparently been very largely decreased. Still the net gain the past four years has been 8,259. This probably does not allow for the entire gain. There has been considerable smuggling in of coolies. Other evasions of the exclusion laws, such as the bringing in of "minor children" by the present residents, have been the subjects of notice in the reports of the Philippine commission. Companies and firms have existed at the principal ports of China for the express purpose of aiding the emigrant to gain a footing on the shores of the Philippine "el dorado" by hook or by crook. Thus, while the government figures place the present number of Chinese residents at 56,000, the consular and other estimates are much higher, ranging up to 62,000. The 1908 report of the Philippine commission admits that the exclusion laws have *not decreased* the

Chinese population, nor even held it stationary. There has probably been some slight decrease, estimated at 3,000, in the city of Manila, but in the provinces the Chinese have much more than doubled their number in the last ten years.

As to the Oriental immigrants other than Chinese, the greatest number since American occupation have been Japanese, the number from Japan increasing steadily each year until 1904, when there were 2,270 arrivals, but since 1905 the number has dwindled to less than 400 annually. The Japanese population is not large and seems to be in no immediate prospect of increasing greatly. They have never been a strong element in the Philippines, even in the long period of Spanish rule. Japan's surplus population is just now expanding in the direction of the mainland, chiefly into Korea and its hinterland. ' From the Japanese element of the immigration into the Philippines, therefore, the United States and the Philippine government need not expect any serious problem.

Of the other Asiatics all together there have not been more than 300 arrivals in any one year since 1904, and this would bring us to the conclusion that the net number of these immigrants was very small and practically a negligible quantity. Such as this element is, it consists about half of East Indian races and the other half of all the other Oriental races in isolated and scattering numbers.

The foregoing figures show the predominant part which Chinese immigration plays in any consideration of the problems now existing due to the regulation of Oriental immigration into the Philippines. What then are these problems? Briefly stated, they are as follows:

First, the antagonism between the Chinese and the native races, due, in no small degree, to the ability of the Chinese in all the activities of life and his demonstrated superiority in trade. This antagonism has in no measure been lessened by the American administration, under the leadership of which the tendency has been to elevate the standards of living among the natives and thus make their competition with the shrewd Chinese even more strenuous.

Second, the doubtful good which follows the infusion of Chinese blood into the Filipino race. It is realized that the chief trouble makers, politically and socially, come from the ranks of the mestizos.

Third, the lack of a sufficient and an efficient labor supply for the development of the industrial possibilities of the Philippines.

The reality of this problem has been questioned by many employers of Filipino laborers.

Fourth, a constant and a conscious effort to avoid complicating the work of the exclusion laws in the United States, because ɔf the efforts of those who have first gone to the Philippines in trying to come thence into the United States.

Fifth, the problem of the enforcement of exclusion in the Philippines.

In regard to the antagonism between the natives and the alien Orientals there can be no doubt of its existence as an appreciable element in any analysis of Philippine conditions. From the first the slogan has been adopted of "The Philippines for the Filipinos," and this sentiment has found a hearty approval among the native peoples, or at least among those elements of the native population that are capable of understanding the situation. It has ever been considered unwise as a matter of public policy to force an unrestricted immigration upon the Filipinos, whether the exclusion of those alien races which are debarred, especially the Chinese, is justifiable on other grounds or not.

From the point of view of the future of the Filipino people it is a serious question whether or not it would be of benefit to them to lose racial identity in a process of amalgamation that would necessarily follow from the admission of large numbers of Chinese, for example. Few races are as willing to join in a process of amalgamation as is the Chinese. They are remarkably free from the sentiments, pride or prejudice which in many instances thwart amalgamation when two unequal races are thrown constantly together. Many claim that the infusion of Chinese blood into the Filipino races would materially aid and hasten the work of building up the latter into a strong and perhaps more unified people. On the one hand the progressiveness of the mestizo and his abounding energy is contrasted with the lesser ambition of the native. But the answer to this contention cites the appearance of the worst characteristics of both the Filipino and the Chinese races in the half-breed, and the fact that the chief trouble makers in the recent history of the islands have been mestizos. The hope entertained by those opposed to amalgamation is that the number of Chinese now in the islands is proportionately so small that they will ultimately be absorbed and lost in the native mass without appreciably affecting the racial characteristics of the latter.

The most immediate and pressing effect of the exclusion of the Chinese and Japanese from the Philippines is upon the supply of labor. The natives have had to be taught to work, and although wonderful progress is noted in this regard among the Filipinos, yet there has not been an efficient labor supply proportionate to the demands and opportunities for the speedy opening up of the resources at hand. From all sides have come complaints, from merchants, contractors, manufacturers and from army engineers. The inability to get the coolie, however, has forced the use of the native, the study of his ability and the methods of handling him, and in an increasingly large number of instances with signal success. The dearth of labor supply has not been so much due to the absence of the coolie as to the non-working habits of the Filipinos. There are plenty of the latter to furnish all the labor needed. The exclusion of foreign supplies from the market has forced the solution of the question of native labor, a solution not yet perfected, but withal becoming more and more satisfactory.

One of the most subtle problems which had to be faced in determining upon what basis Oriental immigration into the Philippines would be permitted lay in the effect which such immigration would ultimately have upon the working of the exclusion laws of the United States. Having assumed the government of the Philippines from altruistic and humanitarian motives, publicly proclaimed and many times reiterated, it would be difficult indeed for the United States to apply to the inhabitants of our far eastern dependencies the exclusion laws which applied to other Oriental peoples. An inhabitant of the Philippines, so long as the islands were under our control, could with ill grace be denied the privilege of access to our shores. Many of the Chinese and Japanese in the islands who would otherwise be excluded from the United States might thus secure admission, for Filipino citizenship would be beyond the reach of but few of them. They have often become Filipino citizens. What, then, was to prevent Filipino citizenship from becoming a mere wedge by which large numbers of persons who would otherwise be excluded could enter the United States. This was merely a possibility. The status of the Philippines in relation to the United States had not yet been determined. No one who knows the lengths to which men have gone in their efforts to evade the present exclusion laws can doubt that the work of regulating immigration might have been greatly complicated through the medium of Filipino citizenship, had it been left accessible to all who desired it. This was a problem which was avoided by extending to the Philippines in September, 1899, the exclusion laws of the United States.

As in every instance where a policy of exclusion is adopted there have arisen in the Philippines serious problems involving the enforcement of the exclusion enactments. In the Philippines the question of enforcement reaches its most acute stage. Not only have the usual methods common to this country been adopted but in addition a system of registration has been superimposed. Every Chinese is required to register with the government, or become liable to deportation, even this has not checked immigration. Until 1907 a common method of evasion was by the bringing in of "minor children" by the registered Chinese of the islands. In that year more rigid interpretations of the statutes were authorized and this practice has been minimized, though not wholly stopped. One of its worst features is that many of those thus entered are sold into a servitude that is not unlike slavery.

Besides this more open defiance of the exclusion laws, there is admittedly considerable smuggling of Chinese into the islands. The exact extent of this practice cannot be determined but it has been important enough to call forth repeated and official recognition of its existence. The smuggling is systematized and until about two years ago the operations in China were carried on with little secrecy. The coast patrol in the Philippines can make such smuggling difficult, but no more. Besides it must be borne in mind that the crews of most of the vessels plying between China and the Philippines are composed of Chinese, at least in part, and that not only these seamen often attempt desertion in order to gain admittance, but they are only too willing to aid a fellow countryman in his efforts to evade the customs officers. For in the Philippines the administration of the exclusion laws is a part of the work of the Bureau of Customs.

Notwithstanding all these evasions of the law the exclusion policy of the United States may be fairly said to be accomplishing the three ends which justify its existence. There is no overwhelming of the Filipino race in its development. There is no diversion of that development through the modifying influences of a process of amalgamation with other Oriental races, chiefly the Chinese. No new and unrelated element is added to the already heterogeneous Philippine population. At the same time the Filipino is slowly learning to develop the material resources of the land in which he dwells. The United States, in protecting itself against possible evasions of its own exclusion laws by making them applicable to every part of the territory under its control, has fortunately done only what would have been in any case politic and justifiable because of its recognition of Filipino sentiment. Only a policy of exploitation could absolutely disregard the racial instincts of a dependent people. If with all the advantages of western civilization at our command American standards of life are threatened by competition with the Oriental, how much more difficult it would be for the Filipino race, even under our tutelage, to attain to the same standards which we enjoy and to which they aspire, if we forced upon them the very competition which we fear and avoid! Unrestricted immigration into the Philippines might not prove to be an unmixed evil, given certain aims and conditions, but the present exclusion policy has amply justified its existence as an element in an altruistic administration for the benefit of the native population and it should be continued.

ORIENTAL LABOR IN SOUTH AFRICA

By L. E. Neame,

Johannesburg, South Africa; Author of "The Asiatic Danger in the Colonies."

No student of the Asiatic problem in America can afford to ignore the effects of imported colored labor in South Africa. South of the Zambesi an "experimental plot" has been conducted for many years, and from its records other lands can see what the competition of the races of the East really means, and what influence that competition is likely to have upon a white population. But in glancing at the dismal picture presented by South Africa to-day, it must be remembered that the Asiatic competition to which the people of European descent are subjected, is by no means the worst of its kind. The Indian immigrants in these colonies are usually drawn from the dregs of the millions of India. In energy, ability and the capacity for succeeding they are far behind the Chinese in the Straits Settlements, or the Japanese of British Columbia.

Although in South Africa the native black population now outnumbers the whites by six to one, this was not always the case. In the earliest days of European settlement in the Cape Colony, the newcomers found an almost empty land. The Kaffir invasion from the northeast had not reached within hundreds of miles of Table Bay. The only people found in the vicinity of the settlement were a few wretched tribesmen who wandered over a large area of country. If, soon after Van Riebeek began his garden in 1652, a policy of introducing white labor had been adopted and systematically followed up, South Africa to-day would be a far different country. Only the system of relying upon colored labor has kept it back. The first slaves brought to the little settlement were shipped from Asia. Then the Dutch colonists sent to the West Coast of Africa for blacks, and several hundred had been introduced before the close of the seventeenth century. The system led with great rapidity to the springing up of a half-breed race, and Isbrand Gostic, who visited the Cape in 1671, considered the circumstances so scandalous and demoralizing to the whites that he attempted to legislate against them. In these early days, however, there was no likelihood of the system being altered for sentimental reasons. It was too widely accepted as the most reasonable policy of development.

In 1716 the Council of Policy at Table Bay came to a decision which must always be regretted by the lover of South Africa. The directors of the Dutch East India Company in Holland submitted a number of important points to the Council at the Cape, and among them was the question whether it would not be more advantageous to employ European laborers than slaves. "It must ever be deplored," says Theal, the historian of the Cape, "that of the men who sat in the Council in February, 1717, there was but one who could look beyond the gains of the present hour." Only the commander of the garrison, Captain Dominique Pasques de Chavonnes, a brother of the governor, advocated the introduction of European workmen instead of slaves. But this view was voted down. The basis of South Africa was made colored labor, and it has been the basis of the country to this day, with the result that in this huge tract of land stretching from Table Bay to the Zambesi there are but a little over a million white people—the population, say, of Nebraska. Only one or two enlightened men saw the danger. One of them was the governor-general, Van Imhoff, who, in a memorandum he drew up in February, 1743, regretted that Europeans in large numbers were not sent out in the early days of the settlement. The introduction of slaves, he said, had caused every white man, no matter how humble his birth, to regard himself as a master, and unless paid at an extravagant rate he expected to be served instead of to serve others.

In South Africa the importation of Asiatic slaves went on until 1767. Then the government at the Cape became apprehensive of the too great preponderance of this class of the population—"for when excited they were prone to commit appalling crimes," and the Council of India were earnestly asked not to continue to export Asiatic slaves to South Africa.

In the next century came British dominance at the Cape, and the liberation of the slaves. But the habit of relying upon colored labor had become ingrained, and, as the natives of the country were unreliable workers, it was resolved to import Asiatics.

The beginning of the Oriental labor system in South Africa on any considerable scale dates back to 1859, when the land owners of Natal asked Sir George Grey to be allowed to import labor. The

Corporation of Durban supported the appeal in an address which included the following:

Independently of measures for developing the labor of our own natives, we believe your Excellency will find occasion to sanction the introduction of a *limited number of coolie or other laborers* from the East in aid of the new enterprises *on the coast lands,* to the success of which sufficient and reliable labor is absolutely essential; for the fact cannot be too strongly borne in mind that on the success or failure of these rising enterprises *depends the advancement of the colony or its certain and rapid decline.* Experimental cultivation has abundantly demonstrated that the issue depends solely on a constant supply of labor.

The manner in which this comparatively modest request has expanded in the course of half a century is a remarkable indication of the danger of admitting Asiatic labor. The "limited number of coolie or other laborers from the East" has swelled into an Indian population *greater than the entire white population of Natal.* The Asiatics called in to help industries on "the coast lands" have spread all over the uplands which ought to support a large white population. Instead of the tea and sugar planter alone demanding Asiatic labor, it is the farmers, the manufacturers, the wealthier residents of town and country alike. To-day the adult male Indians in Natal outnumber the adult male Europeans by ten thousand. Indian shops are found in the best streets of Durban, and in some of the small towns hardly a white man's store is left. The "limited number" of coolies now own thousands of acres of land. They are the fruit and vegetable growers of the colony. The Kaffir "truck" trade, which at one time supported many white families, has drifted almost entirely into their hands. A member of the Natal Legislature wrote some time ago:

Indians both rent land and hold it freehold, and their holdings of both classes are extending year by year. Large areas in the coast country of Victoria, north of Durban, have of late years been acquired by syndicates of Europeans and retailed acre by acre to these people, who are keen to buy, and are willing to pay prices which no European could afford for occupation and cultivation. As a matter of fact, in this Garden County of the Garden Colony, the European population cultivating or in intimate connection with the soil is probably smaller in number than it was thirty years ago, while the Indian is gradually taking up the land upon which was (*sic*) reared in those days families of Europeans—colonists of the best stamp. What will be the outcome is causing anxious thought to many in Natal, who look beyond the present day and its present profit.

In "The Asiatic Danger in the Colonies"[1] I gave some figures, taken from the Natal Census Report of 1904, showing the extent to which Oriental competition has gained a grip on the colony. As no later figures are available at present, I may be allowed to reprint two of the tables. The first deals with storekeeping:

	Europeans.	Asiatics.
Storekeepers (general)	658	1,260
Storekeepers' assistants	1,252	1,323
Bakers and confectioners	213	78
Butchers and assistants	306	42
Grocers and assistants	425	75
Restaurant keepers	64	26

The second table is a more general one:

	Europeans.	Asiatics.
Bricklayers and assistants	1,056	122
Blacksmiths and assistants	523	30
Barmen	251	37
Brick and tilemakers	98	23
Boot and shoemakers	108	66
Barbers and assistants	118	131
Brewers and assistants	68	27
Bookbinders and assistants	47	13
Billiard markers	33	11
Carpenters and assistants	2,328	196
Cooks	147	457
Coachmen and grooms	92	117
Cycle dealers and mechanics	37	12
Carriers and carters	137	262
Cigar and cigarette makers	11	104
Domestic servants	1,083	2,132
Engine drivers (locomotive and stationary)	516	57
Fishermen	100	108
Firemen and stokers	652	257
Hawkers	19	1,487
Jewelers and assistants	105	381
Laborers (general)	353	13,799
Laborers (railway	164	610
Municipal employees	141	543
Messengers	3	99
Miners	208	185
Mineral water manufacturers and assistants	69	21

[1] Published by Routledge & Sons in 1907.

	Europeans.	Asiatics.
Mine laborers	...	600
Painters	661	79
Printers and compositors	448	61
Plumbers and tinsmiths	356	81
Photographers and assistants	99	12
Porters (hotel and general)	96	133
Pumpmen (Natal railways	1	32
Pointsmen (Natal railways)	...	138
Quarrymen	16	56
Tailors and assistants	266	126
Tobacconists and assistants	47	22
Waiters	100	658

One more example of the effect of Asiatic competition may be quoted, because it shows how, even in times of great depression, the Oriental can thrive while the white man goes under. The Cape Colony, like the rest of South Africa, has in recent years gone through extremely bad times. White storekeepers went under in large numbers. But the Orientals held their ground. For instance, in the five largest towns in the Cape Colony—Capetown, East London, King William's Town, Kimberley, and Port Elizabeth—the number of general dealers' licenses issued to Europeans in 1905 was 5,222. But on May 1, 1906, only 3,920 Europeans had taken out licenses. That is to say, 1,302 Europeans had been forced out of business. Now in 1905 there were 1,012 general dealers' licenses issued to non-Europeans. But on May 6, 1906, there had been no decrease. On the contrary, the licenses numbered 1,059. In these five towns, therefore, in one year the increased competition had had the following effect:

1. Licenses to Europeans *decreased* 1,302.
2. Licenses to non-Europeans *increased* 44.

In the face of these statistics, all taken from official publications, it is hardly necessary to dwell further upon the effect of an infiltration of Asiatics into a land in which there is already a large white population. The figures tell their own tale.

The condition of South Africa—especially of Natal—is a warning to other lands to bar Asiatic immigrants. I have no prejudice against the Eastern races. During several years' residence in India I had many opportunities of seeing the excellent qualities of an Asiatic people—personally I prefer India to any country I have seen. But I cannot shut my eyes to the disastrous effects of allowing any considerable Asiatic population to settle in a land in which there is already a large white population. The Asiatics will never be absorbed. Always they will live apart, a source of weakness to the community. America has absorbed hundreds of thousands of foreigners from Europe. They have intermarried with the older population. Hardly a trace of them will remain in a few generations. But a hundred thousand Asiatics in Natal have not been absorbed and never will be absorbed; and in America the same isolation would be found for generation after generation.

Both economically and socially the presence of a large Oriental population is bad. The Asiatics either force out the white workers, or compel the latter to live down to the Asiatic level. There must be a marked deterioration amongst the white working classes, which renders useless a great deal of the effort made in educational work. The white population is educated and trained according to the best ideas of the highest form of Western civilization—and has to compete for a livelihood against Asiatics. In South Africa this competition is driving out the white working class, because the average European cannot live down to the Asiatic level—and if it is essential that the European must do so, then for the sake of his own happiness do not educate him up to better things. If cheapness is the only consideration, if low wages are to come before everything else, then it is not only waste of money, but absolute cruelty, to inspire in the white working classes tastes and aspirations which it is impossible for them to realize. To meet Asiatic competition squarely it would be necessary to train the white children to be Asiatics. Even the pro-Orientals would hardly advocate this.

Further, Asiatic labor in South Africa is now seen to be a weakness to the state. It drives out white people in a land in which white men are needed for the safety of the community against the Kaffir hordes. It increases the problems of the country by establishing a large colored population which is not native and resents being brought under laws for natives, and yet cannot be placed on an equality with the white population. Besides, the Asiatic is worth less to the country than the white man he displaces. It is estimated in Natal that the Oriental only contributes £1 6 4½ a year to the public revenue, whereas the white resident returns £30 11 4. The Oriental buys as little as possible and sends all he can to his relatives in Asia. If he marries and settles down, his children only increase the difficulty of the color problem.

The experience of South Africa is that when once Asiatic labor is admitted, the tendency is for it to grow. One manufacturer secures it and is able to cut prices to such an extent that the other manufacturers are forced either to employ Asiatics also or to reduce white wages to the Asiatic level. Oriental labor is something which does not stand still. The taste for it grows. A party springs up financially interested in increasing it. In Natal to-day the suggestion that Indian labor should no longer be imported is met by an outcry from the planters, the farmers and landowners, and a certain number of manufacturers, that industries and agriculture will be ruined. So the coolie ships continue to arrive at Durban, and Natal becomes more and more a land of black and brown people and less a land of white people. Instead of becoming a Canada or New Zealand, it is becoming a Trinidad or Cuba. Instead of white settlers there are brown settlers. The landowner does not mind, because as Mr. Clayton, an ex-cabinet minister in Natal, said a few years ago, he was pretty confident that his children, rather than have to work any land he might be able to leave them, would prefer to let it to Indians at reasonable rents. The planters and the manufacturers do not mind, because the more Asiatic labor they can get the smaller will be their wages bills and the larger their profits. But the working class white population has to go, as it is going in Natal. The country becomes a country of white landlords and supervisors controlling a horde of Asiatics. It does not produce a nation or a free people. It becomes what in the old days of English colonization was called a "plantation."

The objection to Oriental labor in a white community is not based upon color prejudice. It is an instinct—the instinct of self-preservation. Instinctively the white community realize that with Asiatic immigration their highest ideals cannot survive. The late Sir Henry Parkes put the case eloquently in Australia years ago, when the white man's country ideal was fought for and won there. "It is our duty," he said, "to preserve the type of the British nation, and we ought not for any consideration whatever to admit any element that would detract from, or in any appreciable degree lower, that admirable type of nationality. We should not encourage or admit amongst us any class of persons whatever whom we are not prepared to advance to all our franchises, to all our privileges as citizens, and all our social rights, including the right of marriage. I maintain that no class of persons should be admitted here, so far as we can reasonably exclude them, who cannot come amongst us, take up all our rights, perform on a ground of equality all our duties, and share in our august and lofty work of founding a free nation."

South Africa sees now that this policy cannot be carried out if Asiatic immigration is allowed. The colonies here are on the point of forming the Union of South Africa under a strong central government. I have no hesitation in predicting that one of the first steps the Union Parliament will take will be to stop the importation of Oriental labor into Natal—even though that labor is from another part of the British Empire. The white people of South Africa will demand this measure. And they will do so because they realize now that the influx of an Oriental people into a white community inevitably results in the ruin of a large number of white families, and in the springing up of difficulties which it were wiser to avoid.

JAPANESE IMMIGRATION INTO KOREA

By Thomas F. Millard,
New York City; Author of "The New Far East" and "America and the Far
Eastern Question."

In modern times immigration may be divided roughly into two classes: persons who come to a country with purpose to establish a permanent residence, acquire citizenship, and adapt themselves to its institutions; and persons who, because of their own disinclination, or from being prevented by laws of the nation, do not become subjects or citizens of the state where they reside, occupying the situation of foreign residents.

Japanese immigrants into Korea do not fall exactly within either of these classes. Indeed, they hardly can be termed immigrants in a political sense, since by moving from Japan into Korea their general political status undergoes no material alteration. They still are Japanese subjects living in a country governed by Japan; and it is improbable that this condition will ever be modified. To-day Japan is absolute sovereign in Korea, and exercises unrestrained all functions of government, although a Korean emperor is presumed to reign and a Korean ministry nominally exercises some administrative authority.

Japanese immigration into Korea, therefore, does not present a political problem in an international sense; and consequently is interesting rather in its economic and sociological phases, from which some conclusions may perhaps be deduced that will bear upon the question of Asiatic immigration into the United States. In this connection, the thesis of Japan's administration in Korea should be considered, for it affords a basis for estimating certain effects of her policy. Obviously, the policy is paternal in conception and operation, in the sense that it assumes that Koreans are incompetent to govern themselves. This is the theory of many similar policies, of which British administration in Egypt and India, Dutch rule in the East Indies, and American government of the Philippines are prominent instances. Of these examples, Japan's rule in Korea is more like Dutch colonial administration; but it differs. in the matter of immigration, from all of them. In the case of Great Britain, Holland and the United States, the paternal relation is exercised by a race not adaptable, in large numbers, to life in the regions thus brought under their authority; and so the immigration of English into India, Dutch into the East Indies and Americans into the Philippines in no way threatens to disturb economic and sociological conditions, nor to seriously affect, except by influence of association and example, the native inhabitants. In respect to their Oriental dependencies, the western nations mentioned have never attempted to colonize them with British, Dutch or American immigrants who would or could directly compete with the natives in their accustomed vocations; and in the Philippines the United States protects the natives against Chinese immigration.

Conditions in Korea are different. The country is very like Japan in soil, climate and natural resources. While various divisions of Oriental races present external differences, and to close observation display some diverse traits, they really involve no greater divergences than do the Caucasian nations of Europe, or inhabitants of different parts of the United States. There is little difference between Chinese, Japanese and Koreans as to general characteristics. Owing to peculiar conditions which obtained for so long, Koreans are somewhat less sophisticated than Chinese and Japanese; and from having lived for centuries in a land of comparative plenty, they have not the industrial capability and commercial acumen which a harder struggle for existence has instilled into their neighbors. Until the empire was opened to foreign trade want was comparatively unknown, and the country produced more than enough to supply the needs of the population. With an area less than that of Kansas, Korea has a population approximately of 10,000,000.

While Korea is well populated, there always was land to spare until within the last few years. Growth of foreign trade, and the consequent exportation of foodstuffs, brought the Korean peasant into competition with his Oriental neighbors, and soon caused his situation to be modified by submitting him to a new economic pressure. He now had to labor not only to meet his own simple requirements, but was for the first time forced to sell his products in a general market. Unused land began to have value, and as the cost of living appreciated, the condition of the peasants, who never had been compelled to practice thrift, relatively deteriorated.

This was the situation when the sovereignty of Japan was established by seizure of Korea, in 1904, and when the tide of Japanese immigration into the country began to swell. There were some Japanese in Korea before the Russo-Japanese War, and they were accorded the same privileges and rights there as other foreigners; yet there never was any great influx. Natural conditions in no way have been changed by the establishment of Japanese rule there. Korea is no nearer to Japan than before. It is somewhat more accessible, in a modern sense, owing to railway communications and better shipping facilities; but for hundreds of years Japanese fishermen have plied Korean waters in their boats, and had conditions tempted them there was no serious obstacle to prevent them from immigrating in large numbers. The reason they did not do so seems to be because Korea offered no especial inducement to Japanese immigrants. A Japanese trader or peasant formerly had no greater opportunities in Korea than in Japan, and so, except some adventurous persons, they remained at home.

An explanation for the Japanese immigration into Korea since 1904 must, therefore, be sought apart from natural conditions; and investigation of the factors involved indicate that politics rather than economics provided the incentive for it. It is a result of a deliberate colonization policy of the Japanese government. The broader purposes of Japan in wishing to colonize Korea with Japanese are almost self-evident, and perhaps are well enough understood to not require elucidation in this connection. Assuming that the Japanese government desires to induce 5,000,000 Japanese to settle in Korea (which is a number mentioned in discussion in the Diet), it must excite among them a desire to go to Korea, and secure contentment for them when they go. In time the success of the plan will depend upon the latter contingent, for unless Japanese immigrants in Korea are satisfied they will not remain, and the project to Jap-ize the country will fail.

Tn creating among Japanese a desire to go to Korea the government employed all of several means which it controls: publicity, the shipping lines and the emigration companies being the more important. The affiliation of emigration companies in Japan with the government, through the subsidized shipping companies, is very close; and when backed by the government, with the advantage of special transportation rates, it was not difficult for them to induce mary Japanese to take a chance in the new country. I have no authentic figures showing the extent of Japanese immigration into Korea during the last five years; but unofficial statistics fix it at 85,000 in 1904, 115,000 in 1905, 120,000 in 1906, and 60,000 in 1907. When I was last in Korea, in 1908, the number of Japanese in the country was estimated at less than 500,000. The high-water mark of this immigration was reached in 1906.

The turn of the tide, notwithstanding extraordinary inducements afforded by preferential treatment both in getting to Korea and establishing settlers there, probably caused the Diet to grant a charter to the Oriental Colonization Company, which was organized in 1908 with a capital of 10,000,000.00 yen, and which receives an annual subsidy of 300,000.00 yen from the government in the form of guarantee of interest on debentures. This company has a one hundred year franchise, and is equipped with a blanket charter. The Diet has authorized it to issue debentures for 20,000,000.00 yen, and two members of the ministry were in the company's first directorate.

The charter thus enumerates the enterprises in which the Oriental Colonization Company may engage:

1. Agriculture.
2. Sale, purchase, leasing and hiring of lands necessary for colonization purposes.
3. Undertakings connected with land and its control.
4. Construction, sale, purchase and renting of necessary buildings.
5. Collection and distribution of Japanese and Korean colonists.
6. Supply of seeds, seedlings, fertilizers and other materials for industries to Japanese and Korean farmers.
7. Supply to Japanese immigrants and Korean farmers of building materials, utensils and machinery for industrial purposes; ships, wagons and domestic cattle.
8. Selling, buying, transportation and storing of all things produced by Japanese immigrants and Korean farmers as well as of the necessities of life for them.
9. Supply of funds necessary for colonization purposes.

Supplementary Enterprises

(a) Marine industries.
(b) Mining.
(c) Manufacturing industries that derive their materials from agricultural and marine products.
(d) Other undertakings deemed necessary for colonization.

In the Diet, government deputies stated that the fundamental object of the Oriental Colonization Company is to send skilled Japanese farmers to Korea to reclaim the considerable extent of arable lands now lying in waste there. The charter confines the enterprise exclusively to Japanese and Koreans, and a majority of officers and employees *must* be Japanese. Here is a revival of the old East India Company, with the additional power to colonize on a great scale. While, when interrogated in the Diet, government deputies denied that the charter of the company constitutes a monopoly of any kind of business in Korea, it easily may do so when one considers its relation to the Japanese government and the whole policy of the latter in Korea. It may be said that Korean participation in the Oriental Colonization Company is merely a fiction, and similar to the part played by the emperor and the so-called Korean ministry in administrative affairs.

An idea of the effect of injection into Korea of several millions of Japanese, if the scheme of the Oriental Colonization Company proves successful, may perhaps be gleaned from certain results of the presence of those already domiciled there. That most Japanese immigrants would be inferior to the social average in Japan might be expected, for the better classes of Japanese are not disposed to such doubtful adventure. Japanese in Korea are of all classes, from officials of the superior type to coolies. An argument is advanced that the settling of Japanese farmers upon land that is now unproductive will develop the country. So it might; but it appears that of the half a million Japanese who have come to Korea since Japan took the country less than three thousand are engaged in agricultural pursuits. When last in Seoul I made inquiry about this matter, and obtained from as reliable and unprejudiced a source (not Japanese) as I could find the following estimate of occupations of Japanese immigrants:

1. Officials   5,000
2. Traders (including peddlers, merchants, etc., with their families).. 100,000
3. Artisans (including their families) 50,000
4. Coolies 100,000
5. Prostitutes 10,000
6. Miscellaneous 50,000
7. Subordinate government employees, police, etc. 10,000
8. Agriculturists   2,500

Within the last two years a large number of Japanese have returned to Japan, which probably accounts for the discrepancy between the total of this estimate and the total immigration since 1904. This estimate does not include the Japanese military. A striking result of Japanese administration is that the number of Japanese officials and employees in the Korean government now exceeds the Koreans, who are being removed from even the meanest occupations to make way for Japanese. What probably will impress the sociological student in this estimate is that the Japanese immigration is of a character directly to compete with the native population. Instead of opening new avenues of production, this immigration so far merely has brought an additional population to live upon the present resources of the country, which means that it has had the immediate effect of accentuating the struggle for existence, and has subjected Koreans to a severe and unfamiliar competition.

The character of this competition can only be appreciated when political conditions in Korea under Japan's rule, and its application to the situation of the natives, are understood; and as I lack space in this paper to give details illustrating this phase of the matter, I will repeat a summary which is included in my recent work "America and the Far Eastern Question:"

"The scope of this work will not permit relation in detail of detriments which Koreans of all classes suffer under the Japanese regime. Bare mention of specific instances which, supported by reliable testimony, were called to my attention during my last visit would fill pages. These detriments may be summarized as follows: Siezure of land and other property of Koreans by Japanese without proper compensation or legal warrant; exclusion of Koreans from participation in commercial and industrial development of the country; subjection of Koreans to abuse and indignities at the hands of Japanese immigrants, military and civil officials; the practical impossibility for Koreans, except in flagrant cases, to obtain justice in issues against Japanese; superior advantages of Japanese over Korean tradesmen and merchants, through preferential treatment accorded by the Japanese administration; debauching of Korean morals by Japanese immigrants, by the introduction of thousands of Japanese prostitutes and by the introduction of pernicious vices, such as opium and lotteries. The detriments thus summarized are not based upon scarce or isolated cases, but are so numerous and widespread as unmistakably to indicate that they are the result partly of premeditated general policy, and partly due to laxity and indifference of Japanese administrators."

The truth is that Japanese in Korea demean themselves not as ordinary immigrants, but as overlords; and this is as true of the Japanese coolie, in his sphere, as it is of the highest official. The average Japanese in Korea assumes the attitude of conqueror, and seems to regard Koreans as an inferior and subject race. Moreover, they are supported in this attitude by the policy of the Japanese government, and by actions of Japanese officials in Korea. Indeed, the plight of a Korean in his own country is now a sorry one; yet, curiously enough, he may not himself emigrate without permission of the Japanese authorities. Recently, acting upon representations of Japanese emigration companies and their affiliated interests, the Residency [Japanese administration in Korea] made new regulations affecting Korean emigration. This regulation is ostensibly designed to "protect" Koreans who emigrate to foreign countries. In recent years there has been little Korean emigration except to Hawaii and Mexico, where it competes with Japanese immigrants in the labor field. The new regulations make it practically impossible for Koreans to emigrate except under conditions which discourage such disposition. To believe that any solicitude for Koreans animates the Japanese government in this matter taxes the credulity of anyone who is familiar with conditions in Korea.

It is probable that this brief criticism of some effects of Japanese immigration into Korea will interest Americans chiefly by whatever light it throws upon its predominating characteristics. Japanese immigrants into Korea are not responsible for the Korean policy of Japan, but their demeanor under the circumstances is interesting and perhaps illuminating. That Japanese of all classes in Korea are, in their attitude toward the natives and institutions of the country, contemptuous, truculent and overreaching is my firm conviction; and as their political and social situation there is favorable, compared to that of Japanese immigrants to western countries, their conduct may afford an insight into what they might do elsewhere should circumstances permit.

THE EXCLUSION OF ASIATIC IMMIGRANTS IN AUSTRALIA

By Philip S. Eldershaw, B.A., and P. P. Olden,
University Law School, Sydney, New South Wales.

In the history of the Australian colonies, now forming the Australian Commonwealth, the frequent recurrence of legislation directed against Asiatic immigrants is impressive. To quote one example, no sooner did the colony of Victoria obtain responsible government in 1855 than a restriction act was passed, imposing duties on the masters of vessels bringing Chinese to Victorian ports. This is typical of the attitude of all six colonies on the subject. Intermittently restrictive legislation continued till 1890, when public opinion seems to have subsided, to awaken again, with renewed apprehension, in the twentieth century—chiefly owing, be it said, to Japan's prominence in the East, dating from her entry into the family of nations in 1899. It is by no means difficult to realize the causes of this uneasiness.

Within a few days' steam of the northern shores lie the densely populated eastern countries, which demand expansion as a result of economic and other social forces. There are three whose inhabitants are represented in our alien population (which does not, however, exceed 5 per cent of the total). These are India, China and Japan, which together have a population of 715,000,000 people. The following table is eloquent in its possibilities:[1]

Country.	Population to square mile.	Total population (approximate).	Area (square miles).
China	101.36	433,553,030	4,277,170
India (Brit.)	213.27	231,855,533	1,087,124
Japan	266.84	50,841,562	190,534
Australia	1.46 { in 1901 / now about	4,347,037 / 5,000,000 }	2,974,581

It is only of recent years that the true position of affairs has been apprehended by the mass of the people; this tardy recognition being mainly due to the isolation of Australia from world politics.

[1] Official Year Book Commonwealth, No. 2.

But even from the first, hidden under economic and other reasons, there has been an instinctive idea that to allow Asiatics to obtain ¹a footing on the continent would be fatal. Twelve thousand miles from the parent and, at present, protecting state, the full recognition of the problem or rather the crisis has been seen in late years in the feverish desire for the desirable immigrant,—the white who is quickly naturalized under laws suitable to the situation in which we find ourselves.

State Legislation

State legislation is interesting from an historical point of view, and as illustrating the general trend of public opinion, but it should be remembered that state legislation has been practically superseded by the commonwealth acts to be discussed later. This is true, however, only so far as the state legislation conflicts impliedly or expressly with federal legislation. The power which the Parliament possesses of making laws with respect to immigration and emigration is not an exclusive power.[2]

The first act we notice is the Victorian restriction law of 1855, imposing a fine of £10 on the masters of ships bringing Chinese passengers to Victoria, for every Chinese landed. These provisions were afterwards adopted by South Australia in 1857, and by New South Wales in 1861, to be soon afterwards repealed owing to pressure by the British colonial office. In 1877 Queensland adopted practically the same act, with the further imposition of a poll tax, in 1884, of £50 to be paid by each Chinaman. Meanwhile the other five states had passed exclusion laws limiting the number of Chinese allowed to land from a vessel to the proportion of one to every hundred tons burden. These provisions were generally disregarded till 1888, when a sudden influx of Chinese took place, and popular apprehension grew. Several boat loads of Chinese immigrants were prevented by force from effecting a landing at Sydney and Melbourne. An intercolonial conference was held the same year and affirmed the general principle of the exclusion of Chinese and the desirability of uniform legislation on the subject. Exclusion bills were rushed through the various colonial parliaments. To take the New South Wales act as typical, the following provisions are prominent:

²Constitution Act, sec. 51, ss. XXVII.

1. The poll tax was raised to £100.

2. No ship to carry Chinese passengers in the proportion of more than one to every 300 tons burden.

3. The penalty on shipmasters for a breach of this law was £500.

This marks the end of anti-Chinese legislation, chiefly because the end of the acts had been attained; the inflow of Chinese had practically ceased in 1901. In the census of 1891 their numbers had been estimated at 38,000. In 1901 32,000 were the official figures of the number of Chinese in Australia.

Still in the six years preceding 1901 the arrival of colored aliens had exceeded the departures by 5,500. Japanese, Afghans and coolies from British India began to stray through the colonies. At an intercolonial conference, 1895, the desirability of extending the anti-Chinese laws to all colored aliens was affirmed. Attempts were made to do this at the same time in all the colonies (1896), but the British colonial office refused to confirm these acts, despite the important privy council decision in Chung Teong Toy *v.* Musgrove (1891), that a colonial government had the unrestricted right to shut out aliens. The acts were modified and finally passed, the main provision of each being the exclusion of any person who failed to write in some European language an application for admission to the colony. The inadequateness of this test is apparent. An application learned parrot-fashion would not be difficult for an intelligent Asiatic to master. This requirement was not completely amended till later federal legislation in 1901. The penalty for evasion was fines and imprisonment for the prohibited immigrant, followed by expulsion, and heavy fines directed against shipmasters and owners. Two principles seem to have been reached as the result of all these laws, and both have been embodied in the Commonwealth Alien Immigration Restriction Act, 1901. These are:

(1) That the better method of excluding undesirable immigrants is not a poll-tax, but a test of character and education. In other words, complete exclusion has taken the place of restriction.

(2) If the responsibility for undesirable immigrants is made to rest upon the shipmaster or shipowner exclusion legislation will be more efficacious.

This brings the history of anti-Asiatic legislation down to 1901. Its importance has always been recognized in colonial politics. In fact, the necessity for uniform exclusion laws was one of the main factors in determining the six Australian colonies to federate in 1901,[3] and in the first year of its existence the new-born commonwealth embodied previous state laws into one sweeping statute.

Commonwealth Legislation

Under the authority conferred by the constitution to make laws with respect to immigration,[4] the parliament of the commonwealth passed the immigration restriction act, 1901, and the immigration restriction amendment act, 1905. Immigration into the commonwealth of persons comprised in the following classes is prohibited (sec. 3):

(*a*) Any person unable to write out at dictation by an officer a passage of fifty words in length in any prescribed language.

(*b*) Any person likely to become a charge upon the public.

(*c*) Any idiot or insane person.

(*d*) Any person suffering from an infectious or contagious disease.

(*e*) Any person who has within three years been convicted of a non-political offence, or has been sentenced to imprisonment for one year or more or has not served sentence or received a pardon (sec. 3).

(*f*) Any prostitute or person living on prostitution of others (sec. 3).

Exceptions.—To these restrictions there are exceptions:

(*a*) Any person holding a certificate of exemption.

(*b*) Members of King's regular forces.

(*c*) Master and crew of any public vessel, of any government.

(*d*) Master and crew of any other vessel during its stay in port, provided that if it be found before the vessel leaves the port that a member of the crew who in the opinion of the officer administering the act would have been a prohibited immigrant but for provisions of this section, is not on board, shall be deemed to have entered the commonwealth as a prohibited immigrant, until the contrary be proved.

(*e*) Any person duly accredited to the commonwealth by any other government.

Certificates of Exemption

Certificates of exemption from provisions of the acts are to be expressed as in force for a specified period only and may at any time be cancelled by the minister for external affairs. Upon ex-

[3] See Report of Intercolonial Convention, 1897.
[4] Constitutional Act, sec. 51, ss. XXVII.

piration or cancellation of such certificate the person named therein if found within commowealth shall be treated as a prohibited immigrant and deported (sec. 4); an exemption from dictation test is given to persons five years resident in the commonwealth (sec. 4a).

Liability of Masters and Owners of Vessels

Masters, owners and charterers of any vessel from which a prohibited immigrant enters the commonwealth shall be jointly and severally liable to penalty of £100 for each such immigrant (sec. 9). The minister for external affairs may authorize the detention for safe custody of a vessel from which a prohibited immigrant has entered the commonwealth; the vessel may be held for security, but may be released on security being given for payment of penalties which may be inflicted; in default of payment the vessel may be sold (sec 10). Masters of a ship in which a prohibited immigrant comes to the commonwealth shall provide a return passage to such (sec. 13a).

Evasion of Act by Immigrants and Others

Any immigrant who evades an officer, or enters the commonwealth at a place where no officer is stationed if thereafter found in the commowealth may be required to pass the dictation test, and failing, be deemed a prohibited immigrant (sec. 5). Any person may within one year of entering the commonwealth be required to pass the dictation test. Presumption of proof is against such person. Every prohibited immigrant entering or found within the commonwealth in evasion of act shall be guilty of an offence and upon conviction shall be liable to imprisonment for six months, and to be deported from the commonwealth, though imprisonment may cease for purpose of deportation, or if offender finds two sureties of £50 for leaving the commonwealth within one month (sec. 7). Any person wilfully assisting another to contravene a provision of this act is guilty of an offence (sec. 12).

General Provisions

An immigrant unable to pass the dictation test may be allowed to enter the commonwealth on the following conditions:

(a) Depositing £100 with officer.

(*b*) Receiving within thirty days of deposit a certificate of exemption.

Failing to receive certificate he must depart from the commonwealth when deposit shall be returned, otherwise deposit may be forfeited and he be treated as a prohibited immigrant (sec. 6). Any person other than a British subject convicted of violence against the person shall be liable at the expiration of imprisonment to be required to pass the dictation test, and failing shall be deported from the commonwealth as a prohibited immigrant (sec. 8). Any member of the police force or any customs officer may take necessary legal proceedings for enforcement of the act. Police may arrest without warrant a suspected prohibited immigrant (sec. 14). Where no higher penalty is imposed for an offence by this act, the penalty is to be £50 fine or six months imprisonment (sec. 18). The governor-general may make regulations empowering officers to determine whether any person is a prohibited immigrant (sec. 16).

The validity of the above acts as a whole was upheld in the case of Robtelms *v.* Brennan,[4] where the high court of Australia laid down that every state can decide what aliens shall become members of the community. This case further decided that every state had an unqualified right to expel or deport (see sec. 7 of act) as well as to prevent entering. The right can be exercised in whatever manner and to whatever place necessary for effective deportation.

A survey of the text of the acts as above would seem to show that the commonwealth parliament had only provided against the influx of uneducated or criminal persons, but a glance at one section of the act of 1901 and at its general administration will show that it is particularly directed against Asiatic immigration.

Thus the act of 1901 laid down a dictation test in any prescribed *European* language. So all Asiatics, save those acquainted with the European language were excluded. In point of fact only thirty-two Asiatics passed the test in the years 1902, 1903, 1904. In the act of 1905 the test was altered to be "in *any* prescribed language." The alteration was undoubtedly made with a view to remove a direct expression of offence against Asiatic peoples. This was the more necessary as British policy in the far East was and

[4] C. L. R. 895.

is centered round a treaty of alliance with Japan. But the exclusion of Asiatics has since the 1905 act really been more rigid than under that of 1901. Only one native of Asia passed the dictation test in 1905 and none have passed it since. The explanation lies in the fact that no regulations have been made, as provided for under sec. 16, for the guidance of officers in deciding who are to be deemed prohibited immigrants. The officers administering the act have authority from the case of Chia Gee v. Martin.[6] There the high court of Australia laid down the important principle that it is for the officer and not the immigrant to select the European language for the dictation test; and although as noted above the act of 1905 alters the words "any European language" to "any language" it would seem that the decision would still hold good with respect to the choice of language resting with the officer. Thus at discretion he can exclude any immigrant whatever, even European—and of Asiatics educated as well as uneducated. At the present moment it is a matter of deepest offence to eastern races that no distinction is made in favor of those who represent their highest civilization.

As further illustrating the large amount of discretion allowed officers in the administration of the acts is the case of Prestor. v. Donohue.[7] In this case it was held that an officer having applied himself to the relevant question as to whether a member of a ship's crew found absent before the vessel clears the port is a prohibited immigrant, his opinion could not be questioned in a prosecution founded on that opinion.

As a principle of policy this discretion allowed to officers has always been exercised for the stringent exclusion of Asiatics. In this connection the case of Ah Yin v. Christie[8] is worthy of note. This decided that an infant born out of Australia, and who has never been here and is the son of a person domiciled in Australia, is irrelevant to the question whether that infant on coming here is a prohibited immigrant within the meaning of the acts.

The final proof that it is the policy of Australia to exclude Asiatics is afforded by the provisions of the naturalisation act of 1903. By this act an applicant for a certificate of naturalisation in the commonwealth must adduce evidence to show that he is not an

[6] 3 C. H. R. 649.
[7] 3 C. L. R. 1089.
[8] 4 C. L. R. 1428.

aboriginal native of Asia (sec. 5), provided that he has not already been naturalized in the United Kingdom, and even in this case the governor-general of the commonwealth may withhold such certificate on the grounds of public good (sec. 7). Since this act came into force, January 1, 1904, not one native of Asia has been naturalized in Australia. The legislation of the Australian parliament on the question of Asiatic immigration has therefore gone farther than that of the colonies which now form the commonwealth.

Questions of external affairs generally and that of immigration particularly present two aspects to Australian statesmen. There is the imperial aspect; the empire extends over diverse nationalities, including Asiatics, for example, natives of India; her foreign policy necessitates friendship with Asiatic races, for example, the treaty with Japan 1906. On the other hand, there is the local aspect; Australia is in proximity to the nations of the far East with their teeming populations, while her own scanty population is almost exclusively of European origin. That local needs have been provided for, even at some expense to those of an imperial nature, is immediately due to the added prestige which attaches to the commonwealth, as contrasted with disunited Australian colonies. At the bottom it is due to the greater freedom which is gradually being allowed by Great Britain to those of her dependencies which have been endowed with a large measure of responsible government.

Reasons for Legislation

The reasons for such drastic legislation fall naturally into three groups. (1) Physiological, (2) Economic, (3) Political, chiefly from the aspect of defence.

1. *Physiological.* With the examples of the two Americas before our eyes no other object lesson is needed to impress the Australian mind with the undesirable result of a land inhabited by people of two different colors. The mixture of one European nation with another may have a tendency for good, the faults of one species may be corrected by the infusion of foreign blood, and the result of such alliances may be virile and progressive. But in every case the outcome of the union between European and Asiatic or European and African has been a generation with the faults of both and the virtues of neither. If ever a great body of aliens

become domiciled in Australia, either to the north or south, two conceivable results might happen. The two elements might coalesce, as in the case of the hybrid communities in South America with fatal results to the individuality and energy which is the birthright of the pure white race. Or they would not coalesce as in the case of the negro and white population of the United States of America. In this case the problem of reconciling two antagonistic races to live in peace and fellowship is one which strains the best statesmanship. Even under the best rule occasional outbreaks would and do occur. Neither of these alternatives commends itself to a community whose alien population does not exceed at present 5 per cent of the total. Hence it is that every effort is made backed up by public opinion to administer the restriction acts as strictly as possible.

In all great cities the miserable mongrel springing from white and yellow is seen, and even now in the slums of Sydney, Melbourne and Brisbane he can be found, though but one in fifty of the small Asiatic population has a white mate. It is in the south, however, that there is cause for alarm. The north of Queensland, and the whole of the northern territory of South Australia have but a very sparse population of whites, a vast and for the most part fertile territory, and a dangerous proximity to Asiatic neighbors. There the physiological problem has manifested itself. There also to some extent the aboriginal native of Australia enters as a factor. Elsewhere, however, he may be ignored as an element in the nation's problems owing to his fast diminishing numbers. Every healthy community has the power of absorbing a certain number of these undesirable crosses, and apparently that is what is happening to the few half-breed children in the segregated aboriginal camps.

But the beginning of a hybrid race with all the vices and physical infirmities of the eastern coolie race is visible in the far northern corner of the continent, having its origin in the time before the immigration restriction acts. The Malay, Filipino and Japanese have crossed with Australian aboriginals. White half-castes have bred with Chinese, Malays and Manilamen, until the low type of humanity which results is dignified by the name of mongrel. But all these considerations have been rather instinctive and innate, than explicit in prompting anti-Asiatic legislation. Those most emphasized have been reasons of economic and of political expediency.

2. *Economic.* This phase of the question of Asiatic immigration is viewed with peculiar interest by Australian statesmen. Their fear of the lowering of the standard of living is perhaps more acute than that of the statesmen of other countries by reason of peculiar natural circumstances.

In the first place with an area of 2,975,000 square miles the density of Australian population is only 1.46 persons per square mile, in comparison with Japan with a density of population of 266.84, British India with a density of 213.27 and China with a density of 101.36.[9] Such figures show that an unrestricted inflow of Asiatic labor would be fatal to Australian industrial interests. Secondly, not only the rate of remuneration of labor in Australia is high—as it should be in any new country, but the prosperity of the wage-earners has been increased by legislative experiments of a socialistic tendency in some of the states at least. Under systems of compulsory arbitration in industrial disputes, and of wages boards where employers and employees confer together under impartial presidents to regulate powers and conditions of work, strikes of any length or importance have almost ceased, and the interests of the wage-earning class are being carefully safeguarded.

Thus an inflow of cheap labor must be most carefully guarded against. A good deal has been said, however, in favor of colored labor being utilized in the tropical parts of Australia, which include more than two-fifths of the continent. But it is particularly for the cane-growing districts of Queensland and the northern territory of South Australia that colored labor has been advocated. It would seem, however, that labor of this description is not indispensable. By the Pacific Islanders laborers' act, 1901, the gradual deportation of Polynesians was ordered. At the same time a bonus was paid on white-grown sugar. As a result the production of sugar in the commonwealth has grown[10] and white labor is replacing the colored with no disastrous effect to the farmer.

It would seem that in tropical Australia there is no absolute need of colored labor—save in the pearl fisheries on the northern coasts, which only produce about £300,000 worth of shell annually.

[9] Including dependencies, Official Year Book of Australia, 1901-08.
[10] Official Year Book of Commonwealth, 1901-08.

Thus the general policy of the commonwealth seems justified. The careful regard paid to the retention of a high standard of living is seen in the contract immigrants act, 1905, which applies even to white labor. This act, in substance, provides that where immigrants enter Australia under contract, this contract must be in writing, and its terms approved by the minister for external affairs. The contract must not be made with intention to affect any industrial dispute; and remuneration of the contract immigrant is to be as high as the current wage. The penalty for abrogation of provisions of the act is £5 to the contract immigrant and £20 for the employer.

When such care is taken of the interest of Australian wage-earners as against the white immigrant desirable in every way but that he is under a contract to perform labor, the exclusion of colored aliens on economic grounds is at least part of a consistent policy. When the low standard at which Asiatics can live is borne in mind the policy seems justified.

3. *Defence.* This aspect of the question is a vital one. The need of an adequate system of defence was a principal factor in the movements which led to the foundation of the commonwealth. Australia, by reason of her geographical position, has in the past been ;outside the center of world politics. But there is every reason to believe that in the future the Pacific Ocean will be an important sphere of international activity and rivalry. America has recognized this; Japan has become a first-class power; China is awakening from the sloth of centuries, and Australia, with vast undeveloped territory, with a coast line of 11,310 miles, lies close to the rising nations of the East. Up to the present she has relied for immunity from attack upon Great Britain, at least as to naval defence. The question of establishing a navy is now prominent in the minds of our statesmen, a question the importance of which can be gauged by consideration of the present naval position of Great Britain in Europe. In fact the first steps have already been taken. If not at this moment, yet in a short time Great Britain will no longer possess the naval pre-eminence hitherto possessed over European powers. This will mean that the security of Australia will not continue to be absolute. She is separated by half the world from England, and from the point where British naval strength is of necessity concentrated. On the other hand, Northern Australia lies

within a few days' journey from the East. Asiatic nations must expand, and Australia, little developed, scantily populated, presents a natural field.

From the nation most in need of new territory for growth, of new fields for commercial development and which can best support its claims by arms—Japan—Australia is secured by the Anglo-Japanese treaty of 1906. But when this expires, when Manchuria ceases to satisfy her the crisis of the commonwealth will come. At present Australia has a land force, including permanent, militia and volunteer arms of 26,000 only,[11] although in a few years a general cadet system supported by the proposed conscription scheme will multiply this force many times. Lines of communication overland between the East and West, North and South do not yet exist, and the isolation of outposts of local defence would be fatal should a struggle occur in the next decade. When these circumstances are considered the policy of excluding Asiatics is justified by Australia's extreme needs. Any immigration that would tend to weaken the unity of a nation small in numbers, holding a territory of vast extent must be prevented.

Conclusion

In pursuance of its general policy of exclusion of colored aliens the Australian government passed in 1901 the Pacific Islands laborers' act. The terms and operation of this act are instructive as indicating the thoroughness with which the principle of a "White Australia" is upheld. It had been the custom in Queensland and Northern New South Wales to employ for varying terms of years the natives of the Pacific Islands as laborers on the sugar plantations. By this act no such laborer was to enter Australia after the 31st of March, 1904, with the exception of persons possessed of certificates of exemption under the immigration restriction act, 1901, persons employed as part of the crew of a ship, and persons registered under the Queensland acts (1880-92), such registration to last five years. None were to enter before this date except under a license. In 1902, under provisions of the federal act, licenses were granted to laborers who did not number more than three-quarters of those returning to the Pacific Islands in 1901. In 1903, licenses were granted to laborers numbering not more than half

[11] Official Year Book Commonwealth, No. 2.

of those who had returned to their native islands during 1902. No other licenses were granted, and all agreements made between natives and employers became invalid after the 31st of December, 1906.

The penalty for persons introducing or allowing a Pacific Islander to enter is £100, recoverable on summary conviction. In all cases the onus of proof that a person is not a Pacific Islander, shall be deemed to lie on the person alleged to be such. Finally under the act officers are authorized to bring before a court of summary jurisdiction a laborer, whom they suppose not to be employed under an agreement, and the court, if he is not so employed or has not been within the past month, shall order him to be deported from Australia. This was before the 31st of December, 1906. After that date the commonwealth minister for external affairs has had power to order any Pacific Island laborer found in Australia to be deported. The provisions of this act are now virtually of no effect, its end having been attained. Deportation did take place in a great number of instances. The test case in which it was decided that such deportation was within the commonwealth power is Robtelms v. Brennan, cited above. This right of expelling Kanaka laborers when exercised by a court of summary jurisdiction under the act is within the competence of the commonwealth. The right to expel implied the right to do all things to make the expulsion effective, and so the right of deportation was not conterminous with the limit of the territorial waters of a state.

As a result, of twelve thousand or more Kanakas which formed the floating population of the cane fields, none now remain. White men have successfully taken their place at a rate of pay, however, which is double that formerly given to Polynesians. To prevent the extinction of the industry an import duty of £6 per ton on foreign sugar was made under the federal tariff and a bonus of £2 per ton on sugar grown by whites in Australia was granted to the planters by act of parliament.

No expense is grudged to keep unsullied the policy, and more than a policy, the ideal of a "White Australia." This, as has been shown, is not a passing ebullition of feeling. It may be not inaptly described as the Monroe doctrine of Australia, only it should be borne in mind that we are acting with reference to Eastern Asiatic peoples only. The Australian continent is not a subject for future colonization and further than that not even for present immigration on the part of eastern races. Any attempt in derogation of this doctrine would be viewed with grave apprehension by Australia, under the aegis of the British empire, and resented as an unfriendly act. This is true even though at present a great part of the continent is far from adequately occupied.